A Fetish for Men

A Memoir by
Dr. Gloria G. Brame

Moons Grove Press
British Columbia, Canada

A Fetish for Men

Copyright ©2015 by Dr. Gloria G. Brame
ISBN-13 978-1-77143-209-2
First Edition

Library and Archives Canada Cataloguing in Publication
Brame, Gloria G., 1955-, author
A fetish for men / by Gloria G. Brame. – First edition.
Issued in print and electronic formats.
ISBN 978-1-77143-209-2 (pbk.).--ISBN 978-1-77143-210-8 (pdf)
Additional cataloguing data available from Library and Archives Canada

Cover artwork credit: Front cover artwork is derived from the 1928 public domain movie poster for *Loves of an Actress*, and is used without malice.

Note: Elements within this memoir have been fictionalized in the interest of privacy and the author's creative license.

Moons Grove Press is an imprint
of CCB Publishing: www.ccbpublishing.com

Moons Grove Press
British Columbia, Canada
www.moonsgrovepress.com

"Gloria is unafraid to tackle
the most difficult and forbidden subjects."

- Joseph Brodsky, Poet, Nobel Prize Laureate

⋛ Contents ⋚

Introduction v

Five Things I Learned from Being the
    Child of Holocaust Survivors 1

A Fetish for Men: Red and Blue 21

Then the New Shoe Dropped 26

The Brotherhood of Paul 31

Form Follows Function 41

I Am A Feminist 60

Anywhere Out of My Life 72

Curiouser and Curiouser and Chloe 79

Somewhere Beyond the Sea 96

Child of Anger 100

Platonic Love 110

I Always Expected the Holocaust 121

About the Author 147

❧ Introduction ❧

I was a breach baby.

I always knew I'd land on my feet.

I was born Gloria Glickstein at Beth Israel hospital in Manhattan in August of 1955. My Jewish first name is Gitl, which means "the good one." My last name was originally spelled Gliksztejn – the Polish spelling of a German compound word, which translates to "lucky stone." Put it all together, turn it into demotic English, and I was born "Goodie Luckstone."

On birthdays, my mother liked to remind me that she suffered through a record New York City heatwave to give birth to me, in the age before air conditioning. It was 96 degrees Fahrenheit when she pushed me out. She always said it reproachfully, as if I should have picked a cooler day to arrive. To screw her even further, I was turned around in the womb and came out feet first, like Alexander the Great.

"Do you know the trouble you caused your mother?" Sometimes when she criticized me, she'd suddenly refer to herself in the third person as if I'd feel more sympathy for that other mother than I felt for her.

The obstetrician reportedly gasped when he held me up after the nurses cleaned me, and said I was the most perfect baby he'd ever delivered. That illusion ended when she brought me home. "If only the doctor knew," she said, "how much trouble you'd be."

❧ Five Things I Learned ☙
from Being the
Child of Holocaust Survivors

⌘

Sometimes, people say to me they wish they were me or at least just like me. I always think, wow, really? In order to be me, or like me, you'd need to have felt what I felt and lived what I lived starting in childhood. It wouldn't work otherwise.

One learns an awful lot of things from being the child of Holocaust survivors but I cannot say if they are things any children should have to learn. When you're a kid, you don't judge or analyze moral lessons. You accept them in the naïve certainty that your parents know the truth and wouldn't teach you lies. You see the world the way they see the world and, for an awful lot of people, it never goes further than that. They will believe the things they learned at age five for the rest of their lives, without asking themselves whether those lessons were right in the first place.

My parents wanted to instill in me working class ambitions, strict adherence to all norms, safe social invisibility, and a constant vigilance because, literally at any second, everything you love and care about could be destroyed.

The choices I've made as an adult are an adamant rejection of many of the things I was raised to believe, even though SOME things have protected me and helped me endure emotional pain. It took me decades to sort out the valuable lessons from the ones I wish I'd never learned. They are lessons which formed the framework for my understanding of life, my bible, as it were. Here are the five most important lessons, so you can decide for yourself on their meaning and value.

First, Laughter Medicates Pain

Virtually every tragic experience in life has two sides to it. The true side, which is the reality of the situation; and the funny side, which is the magic pill to relieve the pain of it. This pill was the product of your own brain's ability to come up with a joke no matter how horrific the circumstance. The only restriction was something that just happened. Then you had to wait until it was all over so other people wouldn't hate you for cracking wise too soon.

One time at the dinner table when I was in my early teens, my father told me the story about the time they hid in a filthy hovel outside of Kiev, where they all slowly went mad from hunger. Unable to leave their shelter for fear of detection, they watched one of their friends unravel. He had been so obsessed with sneaking outside to catch a chicken, that he finally convinced himself he was the chicken. He roosted on his cot, and slept underneath it, making clucking noises.

"Did he survive?" I asked my parents. No, they said, he hung himself a week later.

Pause.

"His goose was cooked," my father said.

"He couldn't duck his fate," I replied.

"How could you!" my mother said. "It's not right! He was a sick man!"

My father and I froze. It had been nearly 30 years. Still too soon?

But then she laughed, and we all laughed, and changed the subject.

So that was one lesson: if you don't laugh, you want to kill yourself or, preferably, the fascists who fuck life up for the rest of us. Don't kill anyone: laugh.

Second, Vulnerability is the Enemy

Some of the worst things that happened to my parents happened in the years immediately following the war's end. First was the stunning realization that everyone had died. Since 1939, they'd been chased by Nazi troops and then evacuated and pushed by Russian ones to the furthest ends of the earth – Outer Mongolia – during their starving sojourn across the Soviet Union. They had no idea what was really happening in Europe. They never saw a television. No one had radios. They could barely read Russian. They had heard rumors, they had met escapees, but when they finally returned in 1946, they were overwhelmed with shock and grief to discover their entire families gone, the streets they'd once lived on in ruins and unrecognizable. They couldn't fathom the magnitude of the devastation.

Now they had to survive surviving. They had to survive the guilt of living when the people they loved the most had all died. They had to survive the post-traumatic stress of their own tragic lives in Russia, from the loss of their baby to my father's forced labor in Siberia. They had to survive post-war Europe, which was a flaming mess of wretched lives and crumbled cities throughout the continent. EVERYONE was suffering. It was an entire continent of human suffering and misery and starvation, and my parents had no one and nothing, except the willpower to survive.

And how do you survive when your known universe is in ruins?

"Don't trust anyone." That was my father's advice.

Think about what happened to his oldest brother, he told me. Sandor and his wife gave everything they owned to a nice Christian couple who lived in a rural town away from Warsaw. In exchange, the couple took in Sandor's son and protected him throughout the war, keeping his Jewish identity secret. Sandor's wife died in the camps, but he survived. Upon Liberation, he found his son alive and well in the kindly couple's care, and had his long-awaited joyous reunion.

Sandor's arrival in the small town stirred gossip, though, and locals started whispering that a Jew was there and the little boy was a Jew in hiding all along. Imagine if the Nazis knew their small town had harbored a Jew? They would have all been shot! It was the Jews who caused the Nazis to attack in the first place, they said. The war was all their fault! And so, in their rage and ignorance, they murdered Sandor and his son.

"See?" my father said. "See how it works? This was AFTER the war. He should have brought a machine gun and killed them all. You can't trust anyone," he spat.

Our family mantra was "Never forgive, never forget." My parents often repeated that slogan, the international pledge of all Survivors and their children. They made me promise I would never forget what the Nazis did to the Jews, and ensured I never would.

Dad told me about the time he and my mother were living in Bergen-Belsen. The United States set up a Jewish Displaced Persons camp right where one of the most notorious death camps had been, and the German government was required to provide Survivors with an early form of reparation, i.e. money for food, clothing, bedding, and all the basics they lacked. With that money came privilege, including the ability for the Jews to hire local Germans – now even hungrier than the homeless Jews – to do menial jobs.

"They all acted so nice, so friendly," he said. "They weren't Nazis, they weren't responsible, they had nothing against the Jews. That's what they all said."

One night, there was a huge commotion outside and my father went to see. A terrified German janitor was being held by a group of men. They had discovered him turning on a switch that would have sent too much gas into all the buildings, enough to kill everyone sleeping, they said. As my father described it, once everyone realized the enormity of what he was about to do, and its unbearably cruel parallel to the gas chambers that had claimed so many of their kin, the men kicked the janitor to death.

"He deserved it. He wanted to gas us," my father shrugged coldly, "just like in the camps. He should rot in hell."

I knew what he wanted me to believe. "They" (everyone who was not one of us, meaning people of other religions, races, and belief systems) didn't really like us Jews. When push came to shove, if another Hitler came along, the whole world would turn against us. Count on it, both my parents said. They lived it, they said.

I said, *But America is a new world.*

They said, *There is no new world or old world, there's only one world and this is how it works.*

I was skeptical, even as a child. They were old and broken, I was new and fresh. I saw hope for a better world. There had to be hope or else life made no sense.

They said, "You can't trust anyone. The only ones you can trust are your parents."

But they weren't very trustworthy. I never trusted my mother, not even as a toddler.

Between the ages of three and five, I spent summers at a Catskills bungalow colony with my mother while Dad worked in the city. She often misplaced me – sending me to play unsupervised or letting unknown adults babysit me, sometimes vanishing on me for hours at a time. I toddled around the premises day in and day out never knowing where I should be or what I should be doing with myself, or who would give me something to drink if I got thirsty.

The first time I woke up from a nap to realize my mother was gone, I was around two or three years old. It was so dark and so quiet the faucet's drips sounded like a gun going off. I called out to the emptiness, and panicked. What if Nazis took everyone away while I slept? I bolted out of bed and skittered down the steep stairs to the front lawn. To my amazement, the sun was in the sky. Dazzled by the light, I missed a step. My feet spun over my head and the world rolled around me like a ride. From my whirling ball of surprise, I saw a clutch of mothers run towards me, arms outstretched, their mouths all forming O's of "Nooooo!"

I split my lip pretty bad that day but, as my mother helpfully noted, I survived.

"Don't tell Daddy about this," she said. "It'll upset him."

After that, I stopped looking for my mother when she vanished.

Once, when I was four, I did the vanishing. I didn't mean to. I'd just done my habitual wandering, only this time I didn't get home in time for dinner because some man took me back to his bungalow and I lost track of the time. When my mother finally located me, she slapped me, screamed at me, and dragged me away by the hand, as if the man wasn't even there. She yelled for hours afterwards. I didn't know what was going on. It was just another day to me until her outburst. The man, whoever he was, wasn't the first person to casually adopt me for a few hours or take me home. I fell in with whoever showed interest, whether they were kids my age, random adults, or the family who invited me to eat cantaloupe with them one day. I never told my mother where I went and she never asked. When I was back with her, she acted as if we'd never been apart all day long.

But this time, when I had left her waiting instead of the other way around, this was completely different. It made me a very bad child. How could I hurt her like that by disappearing, what kind of a monster was I to upset her so much, didn't I know what she'd lived through? Was I trying to kill her? And not just her. It would kill my father if she ever told him what happened.

I didn't actually know what had happened, or why we had to hide it from my father, but the lesson was clear: my parents weren't there to protect me. They were the ones who needed protecting. They expected me to know better, to protect them from tragedy not to cause one. They were fragile. They could break at any time. I had to be stronger than them or terrible things would happen.

My mother never should have had a child but she didn't know that. I did know, even as a child, not so much in my head as in my gut. I didn't like her. She could never make anything better.

"Why can't you fit in with other children?" she always asked me. I didn't know the answer. "Why aren't you more like them?" she'd say accusingly, as if I had deliberately perverted her plan for me to be just like everyone else. "Why are you always reading?" she'd complain, "Go outside and play like other children."

My father was more of a mother to me than her. He accepted me. He even seemed to like me and enjoyed talking with me. He always had hugs for me. When I was little, it felt like time with my mother was a prison until my father arrived home from work and set me free with love.

Deep down, I knew that one day they would be gone too. We were all fated to die. It could happen in the blink of an eye. The Nazis could knock down your door tomorrow. Nazis and people like them – ignorant, hateful, backwards – were the inescapable vermin of life. They were everywhere, waiting to crawl out from the scum-packed sewers of human society and shit all over your life.

There was no hell except on earth, and there was no heaven anywhere. Life was about surviving and surviving until you died, and until then, you were on your own. At least I was. I felt, to loosely translate a Yiddish saying, as alone as a finger separated from its hand. No one who really knew me could love me more than my parents, they said, and yet I knew that they didn't love me as much as I needed them to. I also knew that other children got to be children with their parents. I was held to a more Victorian standard. "Stop being childish," my mother told me as young as three and four.

I told myself I was better off being poisoned by the fruit of knowledge. I needed to grow up as fast as possible because being a child was shameful and hopeless – dirty and sloppy, greedy and whiny, out of control. Adulthood was my chance at redemption, a day when I'd be a better person, when I'd be more lovable, and when no one could hurt me anymore.

Everyone who wanted to be redeemed could be redeemed. Hadn't that very miracle happened to Jews who collaborated with the Nazis? There was a stocky little Jewish guy my parents knew who was rumored to have been a kapo in a prison camp. Whatever happened during the war years, he now fit invisibly into the world of Jewish Survivors. He didn't dare criticize the man out loud but privately, my father said he would have died before helping the Nazis. I knew it was bluster. He was never in a camp. Who knows what a person will do to stay alive when the moment comes? Maybe I would have been a kapo if that's what it took to survive.

These ideas made me pensive and somber and uncommonly forgiving of human weakness. At the same time, it made me hate how emotional I felt, how easily a cross word or nasty look could stab me in the heart. How would I survive life's horrors if I cried when a boy called me a bad word? When a little boy in fourth grade called me a "dirty Jew" I felt traumatized for months. How would I survive a Holocaust if I couldn't calm down about an anti-Semitic slur?

In sixth grade, profoundly inspired by Mr. Spock, I decided I would will myself to be an emotionless, purely logical Vulcan. I'd already mastered the one-eyebrow lift of Vulcan irony and surprise. I'd done the death pinch on several boys who promptly fell to the ground, and even my father had buckled at the knees when I experimented on him. I was so earnest, I had no idea they were playing with me. I thought I could fell a grown man with one pinch of my tiny fingers. I felt invulnerable.

I was now bucking for the total Vulcanic transformation. I planned it carefully, and the following day, managed to maintain a monotonous tone of voice, terse responses to everything, and neither smiled, retreated, nor showed great enthusiasm. It was agonizingly difficult for me, but I kept going. I was sure everyone around me would start wondering why I'd turned into a kind of robot, but no one, not even my parents, noticed that I walked around like a creepy little ghoul for three days.

My experiment failed but it showed me that I could conceal my true feelings from the world. First, no one was paying that much attention to me in the first place. More importantly, I had an amazing capacity for duality. I could hide the real me in plain sight. People saw me but they never really knew who they were seeing. It gave me a mad sense of confidence. It felt like the next best thing to genuine invulnerability.

I reframed my father's lesson on trust.

People weren't the enemy.
Vulnerability was the enemy.

It was okay to hope someone would come through for you but I couldn't hate them for failing. They had their own reasons, their own histories, and their own weaknesses. When my parents hurt me, it was because they couldn't help themselves. I couldn't hate them for being weak. If strangers hurt me, I had no one but myself to blame for allowing myself to be vulnerable in the first place.

Besides, I could take more emotional pain than other people could bear. I was trained for a Holocaust. I understood more about horror than most kids could. While they dreamed of Santa, in my dreams bombs fell and sirens shrieked, and cities fell and people burned alive.

All I had to do was act emotionally invulnerable. If I could only use my logical mind, I would be able to survive anything.

Third, Real Life is in the Shadows

Hanging on the wall immediately outside the close-set bedroom doors of my parents' narrow house was a formal family portrait of my mother's family of nine kids and their parents, ca. 1923. Of the huge brood depicted, and the many children her siblings bore over the next 16 years until the Nazis marched on

Warsaw and changed reality for the Jews, only my mother had survived.

I passed the dead on the way to the bathroom and the kitchen and the front door, and their bright, sober eyes followed me – the grandparents I'd never met, the aunts and uncles I'd never known. It wasn't JUST that they were dead. As every child of Holocaust Survivors cannot forget, they were wrenched out of their happy lives and tortured to death. Tortured and exterminated like cockroaches. Just for being born Jewish.

It was terrifying to contemplate being killed for the way you were born or where you were born, for how you looked or for the genes you inherited, for things you couldn't control. And there they were, staring at me before breakfast cereal every day, their soft ghostly eyes reminding me that no one was safe from genocide.

No one knew what happened to our relatives, how or where they died. What we did know was that they deserved to live, maybe even more than we did. We owed our lost angels a mystical debt. They had died and we had lived on to have enough food on the table and a new life in a wonderful new country. We were so lucky. And yet... the dead overshadowed every word and gesture.

"You look so much like my sister, Rachel," my mother sighed whenever I passed the only picture she had of her favorite sibling in the living room, which is to say every time I walked into the living room.

"I know, Mom," I'd say.

"Only she was so refined. Why can't you be more like her?"

"I don't know, Mom," I'd say.

But I did know. Nothing I did would ever be good enough because no people could ever be as good, as fine, or as perfect as the victims who died at Hitler's hands. They were preserved in the amber glow of my mother's cherished memories. For her, the dead were ever-present, especially when an invidious comparison needed to be made.

Once, only once, did I challenge her.

"Mom, you were trying to be a young Commie and sneaking off to eat pork in Polish neighborhoods, and your parents were Orthodox Jews who kept glatt kosher. Are you honestly going to tell me you never ever had a disagreement with them or that they never criticized you?"

The wild chaos of backpedaling and rage and denial that erupted was not worth it. Of course there had to be fights and arguments and everything else that goes along with being a teenage rebel with Jewish Fundamentalist parents – but my parents had wiped all the bad away and clung with desperation only to their happiest recollections.

I couldn't blame them. It was all they had left. Even their family photos were mere scraps they had painfully collected from distant relatives after the war. Their precious private collection of photos and letters from family had been stolen literally from under them, as they lay sleeping one frigid night in a Russian train station, waiting to be transported to their next destination. I felt like an asshole for trying to make her admit her recollections were flawed.

As for me, I was a big disappointment to my parents. They loved me but they didn't like me. One minute they accused me of acting "too smart" and the next they said I was stupid. They knew my shameful secret: deep down I was unlovable. As I saw it, my parents loved me as much as anyone could and more than anyone ever would, but it was more out of duty than real affection.

It made me love them even more, in a way, because I realized how hard it was for them to have a child like me. I pitied them.

They deserved a better child, a less troublesome one. I'd never be like them, not any of them, and certainly not like the holy dead who stared back blindly as I tried to parse the madness of it all. Who were these people who came before me? Were they really the saints my parents made them out to be? If there had been no Hitler, would Gitl Gliksztejn be sipping *herbata* with them in Warsaw right now, speaking Polish? Would we all be happy then?

Whatever. It was too much to comprehend for a Brooklyn girl living in Sheepshead Bay. Bottom line: the best people were all dead. Ergo, I was stuck with the losers. Our family wasn't going anywhere except a condo in Miami when we retired. Our world was a grubby, narrow passage to death, forever overshadowed by the ugly truth that Hitler bombed open, that a human is nothing more than a fly in the shit pile called life.

My parents' life-lessons were simple: it's all about self-preservation. You do what you have to do to pay bills and eat regular meals. When you get a cozy bed, sleep in it as long as you can. Be frugal, don't complain, cover your ass, and put aside all fancy-schmancy fantasies about life ever being better than it is. Try to be good – to a point. You're no better than the other flies. If you lie a little or cheat a little, so what? If you can get away with something, do it, especially if it gives you a leg up on the other guy. If someone gets hurt, just make sure it isn't you.

Most of all, keep your expectations – of life, of other people – set on low and live quietly in the background of the real world, where the other shadows live. The shadows aren't safe either, but only fools made targets of themselves by stepping into the light. We know from bitter experience what happens to heroes. They die.

Fourth, There is a Hierarchy of Pain

There was never a day in my childhood when I didn't know that my parents had suffered more than I could ever possibly suffer. Even if I lived through another Holocaust, I still wouldn't suffer as much as they had suffered because the only ones who understand how much they had suffered were other Holocaust victims.

Not all survivors told their stories to their children. Mine were talkers. They'd repeat the stories of their war years again and again and again, until they were stamped into my memory almost like I'd been there myself, almost like I smelled the Russian shitholes where they hid, felt their fear of imminent death, and knew the pain of their hunger in my belly. I snickered whenever Mom made eggs, remembering that time in Russia when Dad brought home two prized eggs, the first they'd had in months. He asked for his soft-boiled. She'd never made one before, but undaunted, reasoned that the longer it boiled, the softer it would get, like a brisket. I could not stop laughing at her failed logic, just as Dad had laughed when she served a green rubber rock.

"Do you see this bread?" my father would say as he held up a roll. "Do you know what I would have done for a soft piece of bread when it was 30 below and everything frozen in Archangelsk? I would have KILLED for a soft piece of bread."

I think he would have too. He was a tough guy, my dad.

If I didn't seem interested in the salad, my mother piped up, "Do you know what we ate in Outer Mongolia? Boiled grass! Boiled grass I threw up it was so disgusting. Eat some lettuce."

So I would chew the salad served by a woman who had endured starvation and try not to upset such traumatized people any further. It was my job not just to cheer them up, but to show them that I was the happy child they knew the son they lost during the war would have been if only he had lived. To be anything less was ungrateful.

I couldn't hurt them by telling them that I was in pain all the time. I could not tell them that sounds hurt and words hurt, and even colors could make me feel sick. Sometimes, beautiful things were so beautiful, it hurt, just the way it hurt when things were so ugly that I had to squeeze my eyes shut. Stomachaches and headaches were my normal, and I learned not to complain about them, or about bruises and cuts either, because injuries made my mother frantic. I slept fretfully when I slept at all. Every moment of vigilance lost made me vulnerable to the forces that snatched people away at night.

I knew that my pains, my foolish phobias, my over-sensitivity, they were all so ridiculous, so stupid, so marginal when you considered the Holocaust. Which I did almost every day of my childhood.

When I was six, I made the mistake of confessing to them that something was terribly wrong with me. I thought I was dying. I'd been brooding over it for hours until I couldn't take the fear anymore. I pulled my mother aside and whispered the news to her.

"One of my ears is heavier than the other."

"Talk to your father." She walked away.

I told my father. He gaped.

"Lola, Lola, you gotta hear this." He got my mother to come back, then made me repeat it to them both.

I leaned my head to the right to demonstrate the problem.

"The right ear feels heavier than the left."

My father was delighted, but my mother just snorted and walked away again.

"I'll tell you what you do," my father said. "Lean your head to the left and walk around like that until that ear feels heavy, and then you'll be balanced."

I followed his instructions with a grave face. That didn't work, but I forgot about it by the next day and never had a heavy ear again. That I know of.

Of course I think it's hilarious now, but the pattern of disregarding and laughing at my complaints, big and small, ultimately led me to conclude that speaking my fears aloud made me look like a weak-ass idiot, if not a malicious imp who was deliberately trying to get a rise out of them.

There were a few times when it wasn't funny at all: a cold they neglected until I ended up needing emergency transfusions; a broken nose they dismissed as a nosebleed; and a host of injuries and ailments they didn't seem to worry about. When they could no longer deny that something was wrong, they panicked, smothering me with anxiety, as if I was about to die at any moment. It made no sense to me, and left me unwilling to tell them when I felt sick, never knowing if they'd dismiss my fear or react as if I was dying.

For them, and maybe for all survivors, pain existed on a hierarchy. Real pain was at the top, reserved for the victims of people like Stalin and Hitler. Common childhood fears and pains were at the lowest rank, just above the suffering of an animal. My parents didn't even place their own pain at the pinnacle of the hierarchy. That sacred spot was reserved for the Holocaust Survivors who had survived the worst that the Nazis had to offer, the Jews who went to concentration camps. They were the ones who knew real pain. Maybe someone spent the war years shivering and starving and crapping their pants in fear, but still, they didn't suffer the way someone in Auschwitz suffered. My father wanted me to understand that.

On a long evening walk along Sheepshead Bay one evening, as my father recounted stories I'd heard a thousand times, I asked why he didn't write them down. He'd lived through incredible hardships, including a year of forced labor for the Red Army, building barracks in Siberia under abhorrently dehumanizing conditions.

He told me a story he never told before or again. During his years at the DP camp in Bergen-Belsen, he got to know adorable sixteen-year-old twin sisters who had survived Auschwitz together.

"Beautiful, refined girls," he said. "So sweet, you can't imagine, like angels."

Only 26 to their 16, my father felt a hundred years older than them and took pity on them. He didn't understand how they survived. They were mere children when the war started. They had no parents now, no one but each other. It was a miracle they survived. He quickly invited them home. Over tea, my parents, for the first time, confided their long, harrowing tale of survival in Soviet Russia, while the girls listened sympathetically.

Then it was the girls' turn. They were on Mengele's experiments block, part of the Nazi psychopath's abominable twins experiment. My parents were stunned: they had heard rumors about an insane doctor at Auschwitz who experimented on patients but they didn't want to believe it. The girls now gave them harrowing first-person accounts of their lives as surgical guinea pigs.

With all that they'd lived through and seen, my parents had never heard anything so horrible in their lives. More than that, now that their health was coming back, the girls were so happy to be alive, they never complained about anything. After that, my father said, he could not bring himself to talk about his experiences to others.

"I have no right," his voice trembled with emotion, "NO RIGHT to complain. You understand? You understand what I'm saying? No right. What did I live through? Nothing!" He spat on the sidewalk, as if his own unworthiness was slithering under our feet. "Nothing compared to what they lived through."

The lesson was plain: only Holocaust victims knew what true suffering was about. I was at the low end of the hierarchy and always would be. My pain wasn't even a pimple on the ass of the pimple on the ass of real pain. Kvetching about my lot in life was selfish and deluded.

Fifth, You Never Know How It'll End

One of the most important songs of my youth was a march written in 1943, inspired by the Warsaw Ghetto Uprising. Not only were my parents from Warsaw, but my mother was good friends with Mira Fuchrer, the girlfriend of the Uprising's leader, Mordechai Anielewicz, both of whom perished when the Nazis finally crushed the rebellion.

The song was the anthem of the Jewish Partisans, the rebel fighters who made survivalist camps in the forests of Europe and launched guerrilla attacks on Nazis. After the war, it became an international anthem for Survivors and their children.

The "Partisaner Lid" (Partisan's Song) opens "zog nit keyn mol, az du geyst dem letstn veg," which loosely means "never say that you've come to the end of the road."

That summarizes the message of my youth. Just. Keep. Going.

When you don't have the strength to go another step, crawl if you have to, but die trying.

When you think your heart is breaking, think of something else. What's a heart? Fuck your heart, you don't need it to live.

When the world caves in on you, become your own cave and hide inside until it's safe to go out again. If you have to stand at the door with a club to kill people who try to break in, that's what you do. In fact, my father did just that in another sordid Russian hidey-hole when local Cossacks got wind of some Jews in town and treated them to a pogrom. The men in my parents' squat armed themselves with whatever they could find and leaned out the windows to bash Cossacks in the head until they left.

If you almost died today, thank God you're still alive! What more do you want? You lived. Be grateful. You have another night to enjoy. Eat something.

You can't predict how the story of your life will turn out. Maybe you'll die like a rat in a sewer, maybe you'll end up in a new country with a new life and a big house. There's no plan for your life. There's just chance and your determination to survive.

Who could ever imagine, for example, that the pampered daughter of a wealthy Jewish family, who had never had to do anything for herself, not button her own dress nor butter her own toast, could survive a war by hiding in cemetery crypts, creeping out at night to do whatever it took to feed herself and her daughter, whether it was trading favors with soldiers or hunting for rats. That woman, a friend of the family, lived to reclaim her life of fine silks and furs thanks to a lucrative post-war marriage.

Or imagine sitting at the table, chatting convivially with a bunch of Survivors, when the lady next to you reaches for the bread and there are blue numbers tattooed on her forearm. You know what those numbers mean. She was in a concentration camp. She was numbered like inventory, and scheduled for ex-termination. And she keeps chatting merrily, because even though once upon a time she suffered incomprehensible torment, in the here and now she has a killer recipe for noodle kugel.

In my parents' circles of Survivor friends, there were people who never dirtied their hands and people whose hands were never clean, people who held together and others who crumbled in the wreckage of war. Some survived by sucking Nazi cock and washing Nazi floors, and others bravely endured the Nazi horror machine, defiant to the end. Time was the great equalizer. They had survived to build new families and set down new roots. Whatever went before, now they loved new children and led new lives with new husbands or wives. They forgave each other more readily than they forgave themselves for what they did to stay alive.

Life disappoints, yes. Life corrupts and kills. But life surprises and heals, and life brings miracles too. The only way to find out where you will end up is for you to survive.

❧ A Fetish for Men ❧

⌘

The streets were made of men,
the nights were lit by sex,
I could not scale the walls
from the abyss of myself.

Red and Blue

My first real boyfriend, the first one I was really serious about, was Paul.

When I first kissed Paul, I thought he could be the boy I'd stay with and love for years. I never imagined staying forever with anyone, but I saw no reason why we couldn't always be friends and fuck buddies. He was different from everyone I knew – smarter, more cynical, funnier, and sexier too. Wherever we went, he always had an arm draped around me, always whispered sexy things to me, and stopped often to kiss me. Though he was six years older than me, already in graduate school while I was just a high school senior, he wasn't embarrassed to let people know I was his girlfriend, no matter where we went.

I loved Paul's body. It was boyishly slim, without a waistline, and he had long legs and a smooth chest. Whether by blood (he was Sephardic or Syrian, something swarthy with an S) or uniquely because of his penchant for lying in the sun for hours at a time, his skin was the color of dried almond leaves. Only the bathing-suit-protected skin around his genitals and on his ass showed his true color, a pale caramel.

His hair was perfectly straight and nearly black as an Asian's, and he wore it long, I think, so he could throw it back dramatically when making important statements. He had the kind of face that could, at moments, look ruggedly handsome and then, from another angle, look ratty and mean. He had a sharp nose, slender feet, a short cock, and small, soft hands, like a woman. There was something reptilian about him, but I liked it. Everything about his unusual appearance turned me on, and his small cock looked perfect on his taut, linear body.

I threw myself in with him, enthusiastically. When conversation was good, it was great. He was very serious about his grad studies and very cynical about life, which made him like a nerdy bad boy, which turned me on even more. We usually met on the beach, where he headed after his college classes ended to soak up rays until my high school classes ended a few hours later. One day, I was running late and pedaled fast as I could because I had a weird premonition something was wrong. I knew he would be there, waiting, because he was always there, waiting in a neon bikini so I couldn't miss his ass, but sometimes he got anxious when I was late.

As I walked the bike over to "our spot," I saw a mutual friend squatting over him, looking perturbed. When she saw me, she waved urgently, then walked away fast as soon as I got to them. Paul didn't look so good. He was sprawled on the sand, like he'd had a heart attack and died.

"Paul!" I bent down. He was visibly breathing. "Are you okay?"

"Go," he mumbled.

"Go where?"

He opened his eyes and smiled. "Goria. Hiiiiiiiiii."

"Oh man, you're so stoned."

"Mphmhm."

"Try and sit up, Paul."

"I was waing."

"You were what?"

"Waing. Time is it?" He sank back into the sand. I shook him.

"Paul!"

"Goria," he said.

Down he went again. It was not attractive. It was not attractive at all.

"What did you take?" I knew the answer. He always took Reds. I plopped beside him, and pulled him into a seated position, holding him upright in my arms. "Where do you stash them, up your ass?" I asked rhetorically, since he was oblivious.

Just then, a police officer patrolling the beach walked up to us.

"What's going on here?" he asked. He didn't like the looks of us and I can't blame him. To a cop's eyes, it probably looked like a teenager hugging a naked dead guy.

"He's my boyfriend."

"Your boyfriend?" the cop glared at him. "Isn't he too old to be your boyfriend?"

"No," I said. "I'm a high school senior."

The cop was not impressed. "Well, get your boyfriend off the beach or I'm busting him for public intoxication."

"Yes, officer."

He helped me pull Paul up to a standing position. Actually, it was more like a bent, wobbling position.

"You should find a better boyfriend," the cop said in that chillingly deadpan cop way, like they've seen it a hundred times before and it never turned out pretty.

"Probably." I tried to look cool but I was mortified. Paul being that stoned and nearly naked, helpless and alone on a Brooklyn beach, by his own volition, was beyond my ken. I couldn't understand how he would let anyone see him that way, much less risk a bust. It was Brooklyn, for crap's sake. You don't do that in Brooklyn.

I squeezed myself under Paul's armpit and clung tight to support his weight, puffing and pulling him and my bike through the sand. His legs folded under him every few steps, so it took us half an hour to walk 100 feet.

"What the fuck, Paul?" I kept saying, gasping for air as I dragged his gelatinous body along. "Why do you do this to yourself?"

He regained some coherence when we hit the sidewalk. "I love you!" He kissed me. "I love you so much." He kissed me again, then he kissed me some more, and kept kissing me until I got into it, my desire for him building, my pussy throbbing for him, my nipples aching. I kissed him back with passion and then he kissed me even more and then we left to walk my bike back.

As soon as he found his feet, he got buoyant, singing loudly as we passed through quiet streets, and talking crazy happy bullshit to keep me laughing. Every few yards, Paul kissed me and told me he loved me over and over again.

How could I do anything but forgive him? I couldn't do anything but forgive him. He turned me on too much. His kisses made me drip.

Paul's penchant for barbiturates was but a fly in the ointment of true love. As a pothead, I thought it was hypocritical for me to judge people by the drugs they took. I tried to accept it because, well, hell, it was the 1970s, and everyone was doing one kind of a drug or another. I once spent two hours staring at a lava lamp during an oddly emotional stoner experience. And unbeknownst to any of my friends, my Saturday night ritual was getting completely shit-faced stoned by myself to watch *The Mary Tyler Moore Show*, enthusiastically singing along, "you're gonna make it after all."

So who was I to judge another man's high? Still, fact was fact and Reds turned people into sloppy, stumbly, mumbly-mouthed whiners, incapable of fully controlling their limbs. I forgave Paul for his poor choice of recreational drugs and hoped, one day, he'd see the light and switch to pot only. And hashish. And kif, when available.

❧ Then the New ☙ Shoe Dropped

⌘

He turned me on so much and kissed so wonderfully that it took a few months for me to realize that something was really odd about Paul. Or, rather, something was really odd about his perception of what sex was.

My disastrous virginity give-away fail of the previous year (as detailed in my book *Naked Memory*) left me phobic about intercourse and unwilling to give it another try until I was certain that I trusted the guy and had feelings for him. Paul didn't question me about it, since he was not interested in intercourse. When we were alone in his bare, tiny apartment, he'd pull me down to the bed and spend hours kissing me and humping me with his jeans on, sometimes unzipping his pants to rub me through his Speedo. It baffled me that he wore more clothes to sex than he did to the beach, but whatever.

The first time he ever begged, he begged me to let him touch my tits. This struck me as mildly weird, since I had pulled off my shirt for that very purpose. But I figured it was part of a kinky little game and made him beg a little more before granting him permission.

From then on, it was impossible to go to bed with him without him whining and pleading and mewling. It was amusing at first when he asked permission to touch me or do things we'd done before, because it made our sex feel all new. But then he escalated and started begging for things neither of us had ever even come close to doing together, outrageous, twisted things. Even when the fantasies were hot, I loathed the pressure. It smothered me. It felt like emotional blackmail, like a loyalty test, especially since he withheld affection when I said no.

A deep anger started to grow inside me. I hated being controlled by a man. I didn't want anyone to tell me what kind of sex I could or should have but me. I wouldn't make commitments to his sex fantasies no matter how long and hard he begged. He could beg for hours but I could stay deaf to his pleas for longer, my whole life if I had to. I had received guerrilla training in selective deafness at Mrs. Glickstein's Home for Disappointing Daughters.

His compulsive begging sucked the joy out of our sex life which, in turn, pried loose the rosy lenses from my eyes. I began to doubt my choice to be with him and kept thinking about the cop's advice. I wondered – shouldn't a man of Paul's age and education be able to do better than a pimply high school senior with low self-esteem? He wasn't the prize I imagined. He was a spoiled, fucked up druggie who had to date down.

I didn't notice my patience wearing thin until I woke up one day and, boom, just like that, suddenly realized his abundant declarations of love had diminished to occasional compliments and that he had changed from a happy sex maniac to a whiny control-freak. It's like I woke up and fell out of love. I knew it was the barbiturates that were distorting him, but since I wasn't taking them, I didn't see why I should suffer their debilitating consequences. His whole drug thing now disgusted me. It was ruining him. It had ruined us. I'd woken up from him like he was a bad dream.

Unfortunately, I had a date with him that evening and I felt obligated to go, even though I didn't want to see him anymore. This made me even angrier, because now I was pissed at myself for being stupid enough to honor my promise to see him.

"Do you at least get off on your begging?" I finally snapped. "Because I sure as fuck don't."

He had managed to keep me an hour past the time I needed to be home, and he had done so very deliberately. He had begged for nothing I wanted while my vaginal flora desiccated. I was done.

I pushed him off, sat up on the edge of the bed, pulled on a sandal and looked around.

"Do you see my other sandal?"

"What?" He began softly begging again, "Don't go."

"My other shoe. Where did it go?" I searched under the sleeper sofa.

They were the first nice pair of shoes I owned. They were the softest leather I'd ever touched and had perfect heels. They made my feet so happy. I bought them with my own savings too and was proud of that.

"Where is my damn shoe?" I tore at the blankets and rotor-tilled the sheets.

Paul was pretending not to notice my dilemma and said, "You don't have to go yet."

"I do. Now where in hell is my shoe? Did you hide it?" My eyes went hollow with rage.

He finally began looking around. "Oh no. Buffy has it!" he howled.

Paul was babysitting Buffy, a super-sweet Weimaraner puppy who baby-chewed my hands when I first got there. With her regal blue eyes and silky grey body, I thought she was darling. Until that moment.

Buffy had my shoe, alright. She had it for dinner. She was innocently eating it under the table, its shredded straps hanging from her lips like overcooked spaghetti.

"NO!!!!!!!!!!" I screamed like the girl I was. "Oh no, no, no, no, not my beautiful leather shoes!"

"Oh my God, she ate your shoe. She ate the whole shoe." Paul started laughing. "She ate it down to the heee-heee-heeeeel!" He doubled over, he was laughing so hard.

The more he laughed, the more I hated him. We'd been so engrossed in another tense Beg-a-Thon that I hadn't paid attention to the slurping doggie sounds in the background.

"How am I going to walk home?"

I was defeated. My beautiful shoes. Destroyed. Those perfect little heels I'd saved up to buy at the boutique that had only one pair in my size. I wanted to cry but I didn't want him to see me cry.

"Oh puppy!" I wailed.

"Oh yeah, oh shit, you're barefoot." Paul opened a closet and dug out a pair of flip-flops several times bigger than my feet.

"I'll walk you home, if you want." He tried to look concerned, but as soon as I put the flip-flops on he seized up with laughter again. My tiny girl-sized feet in his man-sized flip-flops were a stunning failure. "Gee," he said. "I don't think they fit."

"Fuck you." I said, "I'll go it alone."

I pushed past him out the door. His gales of laughter followed me down the long hall, growing louder as one or the other thong dropped off my foot. I steamed as I clopped, shooting him death-rays with my eyes when I finally got to the elevator.

When I got to the street, the stupidity of my situation overwhelmed me. I tried walking with purpose, as if it was my custom to waddle along in gigantic pancakes for shoes. It made them fall off my feet faster, so I'd have to double back every few steps. Pedestrians stared and giggled when I hopped off a curb and one thong flew sideways. My mouth froze in an involuntary grin as I skied up Avenue U and I was afraid I'd either have a temper tantrum in the street or start laughing uncontrollably.

After the first quarter mile, I stopped caring. I trudged wearily, stopping every so often to rub the swelling blisters between my toes. I was exhausted by the time I finally got to my parents' door. I threw his flip-flops into the trash cans outside. Fuck flip-flops and fuck Paul.

ɞ The Brotherhood of Paul ʒ

⌘

I've heard that women are lectureful: that they can't let a man go without trying to educate him, yell at him and, to all extents and purposes, annihilate his heart and leave a gaping wound in his psyche.

I'm not that kind of woman. I'm the kind that stops engaging. I figure what else is there to say after goodbye? If someone gets on your tits, and you tell them they're getting on your tits, and they still keep getting on your tits, then you take responsibility for your own tits and get the fuck out of there ASAP if not sooner. And if the guy was a shit-heel, you don't owe him any apologies or explanations.

There's no need to throw salt in his wounds, even if you know exactly where all the wounds are located and keep a jar of salt in your soul for just such occasions. From my strategic survival perspective, one does not up the ante nor does one seek out revenge. You just get the fuck out before the relationship turns into the tsunami that blows your life adrift and destroys everything around you.

I never feared men. I feared myself. When men fucked with me, it wasn't their power over me that made my heart race, it was my rage at the injustice of it. Then I went into my dark cave, the cold place in my soul that nobody knew about, where I didn't feel anything at all. That was my secret weapon: I could be indifferent on an epic level, not caring about anyone, not even myself. I would endure anything to protect myself, including self-annihilation. As long as it was SELF-annihilation, not murder at another's hand, then I won.

Physically I was tiny and feminine, with a Minnie Mouse-like voice and wide smile. It fooled people. No one knew that I saw the Holocaust in my dreams. Self-preservation was in my DNA. I knew what I was capable of. I could kill Nazis and not care. I wanted to kill them and their kind off the face of the earth.

But that wasn't moral. Or legal. So my goal was always peaceful disengagement. I tried to extricate myself gently from the relationship with Paul, calmly telling him that I didn't think we were right for each other. I tried to make it sound like we'd still be friends. I made vague allusions to future dates without setting anything definite.

He was too clever for my ploy. He wanted proof we were still friends. He wanted a favor. He had promised his brother, Andy, that when he came to town, he'd introduce him to me. Would I do him this one favor? He wasn't ready to tell Andy that we'd broken up. He wanted us simply to meet and have dinner, for old time's sake.

He'd told me a lot about his half-brother. I knew he was smart and fun, lived in California, had a successful career, and was gay. The gay part really intrigued me.

I always wanted to meet a real homosexual, instead of the boys I knew growing up who were completely closeted and ashamed of who they were. It seems there never was a time when I didn't know about homosexuals. I can't remember being surprised by it. Men loving men was a no-brainer. Everyone knew men were gorgeous. Naturally, other men would see it too. It was the Age of Aquarius, not the Dark Ages. You could love whoever you wanted to love.

So it felt like homosexuals and I probably had a lot in common, because we both shared the same perspective on men. Plus, I saw them as truth-sayers. Ever since deciding I was a poet in tenth grade, I felt a religious obligation to truthfulness. It was easy to be truthful when you were ordinary. But when you were someone who society feared, so radical you lived in peril just for being yourself, then being truthful really meant something. It meant moral character. Meeting Andy would be like meeting Allen Ginsberg, one of my poetry idols.

So I agreed and we set a date and time for me to come to Paul's place so we could all go out.

When I arrived a few days later, a slight, balding man in his 30s wearing a blindingly bright floral shirt opened the door. Everything about him was like a bad 1970s disco cliché, from the tight bright polyester pants and unbuttoned floral shirt with hair sticking out, to the droopy mustache and pierced ear. It was like he bought the gay disco magazine and copied the gay disco look. I was a little disappointed but chalked it up to living in Hollywood, where garish trends are the norm.

"You mutht be Gloria," he lisped.

NO, I thought, not a lisping gay man. But I sucked it up. Did it really matter? No.

"You must be Andy."

"I've heard so much about you," we told each other and hugged like old friends.

"Where's Paul?" I asked.

Andy sat on the bed, and patted it.

"He'th not coming."

"What? Why not?"

"Wanna come here and get comfortable?"

"Uh," I squirmed, "what do you mean he isn't coming?"

"Would you like him to join in?" He looked a little surprised.

"I thought the three of us were getting together?"

"Ohhh," he said and paused for a moment. "OK, yeah, the three of us. I'll phone him. But don't you want to be with me firtht?"

We weren't even speaking the same language. "Be with you... how?"

"You're Gloria, right?" He looked as confused as I felt. I nodded. "Right. You're Gloria." He nodded eagerly, as if he expected me to know what it meant that I was Gloria... as opposed to, say, Angela or Penelope.

"I'm lost," I said.

"Aren't you here to give me a blowjob?"

I don't know if my head actually flew off my body and spun around the room before crash-landing back on my shoulders or if it just felt that way. "Are you fucking kidding me?"

"Wow, oooh, calm down," he cringed and held his hands up like I was going to punch him.

"What the fuck are you talking about? I'm Paul's girlfriend. EX-girlfriend. EX! What's going on?"

"Ith okay, ith okay," he said, "you don't have to give me a blow-job if you don't want to. I just thought... Paul didn't say girl-friend... well, it's okay, never mind."

He started twitching so bad, I calmed down. "What did Paul tell you about me?"

"Paul thaid a girl named Gloria wath coming by to give me a blowjob," he explained. When he saw my reaction to this, he started backpedaling as fast as he could. It was all a misunderstanding, he said. No doubt, he said. He probably didn't hear it right. Surely he didn't. Perhaps Paul just thought we might get along and want to hook up. Yeah. It was probably more like that.

The more he prevaricated, the angrier I grew. "It's okay, don't worry about it," he whispered, suddenly alarmed.

I wanted to grab his scrawny neck and shake him, crying, "Do I look worried, motherfucker?" but I clenched my sphincter and held my tongue and let him tell his lies and cover his brother's repulsive ass, too stunned to know what to do next.

He didn't want me to feel bad about it. In fact, now he wanted to take me to dinner in the city, to do something fun by way of an apology. He would love to have a real date with a woman while he was in town, no obligations. He hadn't been on a date in months.

I didn't know enough about homosexuals to judge but this puzzled me further. First he wanted a blowjob from a woman, now a date?

"Aren't you gay?" I asked.

"ME??? GAY?!" he screeched like a parrot. "I don't know why people always think that I'm gay, there's nothing gay about me! Do you think there's anything gay about me?"

"What? No," I lied, horrified. "No, of course not."

The more he ranted about how heterosexual he was, the crazier he sounded.

"I gotta go," I said, as he reached for my hands, trying to keep me. I fled. I didn't want any part of these brothers or their sexual neuroses. They were both insane.

I went home in a spectacular state of rage. I nursed it all night. Paul was a bad person. An evil person. He didn't just betray me, he betrayed his brother too. How excruciatingly humiliating for his sexually confused brother to be set up with an uptight feminist who thought he was gay. Paul was a sick prick.

Why did Paul stage this prank? To make me feel like a whore? Why? He wanted to hurt me, obviously. Maybe he thought I'd go along with it, like some bimbo. That hurt even more. But if he thought somehow he had put me in my place, or made me feel guilty and ashamed of my sexually free ways, he was dead wrong. He wounded the outer layer of that dark place I inhabited where everything hurt too much for such a light stab to matter. It only made me hate his lizard-assed body and his oily beady eyes.

Paul lay low for a while after that. As my anger evaporated, I followed my code that the best course of action was inaction. Engaging with him would grant him room in my head again. I wanted him as gone as if he'd never existed. I could do that, relegate people to the trash bin of my mind. So I did. I'd completely moved on when, about 2 weeks later, he called. As soon as I heard his voice, I hung up. He called back. I hung up. He called back.

"Don't hang up, I'll just call back," he said.

I hung up. He called back. I hung up. He called back.

"What do you want, Paul?" I finally answered on his fifth try.

He wanted to see me. I walked the phone to the bathroom and locked myself in to catalogue his betrayals. He waited until I ran out of righteous indignation and resumed pleading. He wanted to see me. Please would I see him? Please? Pretty please? Just to talk? Please?

For the next few weeks, all the begging he once did in bed now switched to the phone. Please come over; please meet him somewhere; please let him visit. When the pleas didn't work, he ordered me to meet him at a specific time and place. I didn't go. He called back to complain and set another time and date. I didn't show there either. But the whole thing was giving me stomachaches.

I knew he was too chicken-shit to actually come to my house and risk a confrontation with my parents. He was deathly afraid that if word of his relationship with a sixteen-year-old got back to his grad school it would hurt him academically. But the tone of his calls was starting to grow menacing. He HAD to see me. I HAD to see him.

"Or else," he'd whisper in a strange tone, though he never explained what "or else" meant.

Paul deserved to suffer. He needed to die. I wished there was a way he could die without me actually killing him. I was past hating him. I just wanted to erase him. He was a rat that needed to be eliminated before he contaminated the global supply of nice women.

Then he crossed the line: he called at 1 a.m., waking up the whole house. I'd been masturbating assiduously for almost an hour, and was just nearing that all-critical pinnacle of pussy tingling that preceded orgasm when the phone rang.

"What is this bullshit, Paul," I growled when I heard his voice. "Goddammit it." Bad enough he was being an asshole, now he'd ruined what had promised to be a fantastic orgasm. "Stop fucking calling me," I hissed.

I turned off my vibrator but left my feet tied so I could get back to business when we were done, as he rambled weepily about how he needed me.

"Whatever you want," I finally said, "no. This is bullshit."

"If you don't see me, I'll hurt you," he said before I hung up on him.

I knew it was the drugs talking, that he probably was too gelatinous to get off his bed, and that he wouldn't remember a word he said by the morning. Still, the calls were making me obsess over the horrible revenge I wanted to inflict on his skanky ass. All the things I used to find sexy about him now revolted me, from his ratty face to his neon Speedo. I couldn't remember why I found him sexy in the first place.

His threats didn't scare me but that he'd sunk to this level did. How low would he go before all was said and done? I sure as fuck didn't want to find out. I wanted him gone. GONE. I should have listened to the cop. Fuck. I should have gone with the cop – he was so handsome in that tight uniform with the handcuffs on his belt. He had more meat on him too. His chest was probably thick with hair, soft dark curls, not like that hairless reptile fuck who was tormenting me.

Just then, my mother pushed open my bedroom door in her floofy pink nightgown. I secured the blanket around me, hyperconscious of my bound feet.

"Who was that?"

"Paul," I said. "He won't stop calling. I broke up with him and he's still calling."

"I never liked that boy," she said. It was the first time she'd expressed an opinion about him. "He doesn't look you straight in the eyes," she said.

The one time I brought Paul to meet my mother, he arrived bare-chested and greeted her expansively, exuberantly, as if she was his future mother-in-law. It unsettled me even more when I realized his nipples were rock-hard as he shook her hand. Now I imagined his sniggering internal monologue, "Hello, I'm here to possess and destroy your daughter."

"I don't like a boy who won't look you in the eyes," she repeated.

"Well, feel good, then, because I broke up with him," I said.

I expected her to start blaming me for my choices but she was too tired. "He shouldn't call so late at night," she said as she pursed her lips.

"No, he shouldn't."

"Doesn't he know you have parents who sleep?"

I'd usually snap off something snotty, like, "No, he thinks you're vampires," but this time, her odd question gave me an idea.

My mother said she didn't like Paul's shady eye thing and if she didn't like something, my father didn't like it either. Maybe I could game the situation. Paul's soft spot was his public reputation. Sure, in private he acted like a stinking pile of shit but his teaching scholarship depended on a pristine public reputation.

"Could Daddy answer the phone next time and tell him to stop calling or he'll report him to his school?"

"Oh, yes," she said. "Sure. I'll make him do that." And with that, she left the room.

I was amazed she let me off so easy. Now I was locked and loaded for Paul. Let him try to intimidate me again, ha! A teenager's father threatening to report him to his school would freak him the fuck out. Oh yes. And the things I knew about Paul, the drugs, the sex obsessions. I could humiliate him completely. Paul would shit himself. I turned the vibrator back on and came like a racehorse in no time at all.

The next time the phone rang after midnight, I heard my father pick up. I carefully lifted the extension in my room and covered the mouthpiece to eavesdrop.

"I'm telling you don't call her anymore," my father was saying, "my daughter doesn't want to talk to you."

"Oh," Paul mumbled, "ok. I didn't know..."

"Now you do," my father said drily.

"Well.... OK!" Paul huffed. "If that's what she wants!!"

And that was that. No-muss, no-fuss boyfriend disposal. He never called me again. He shrank away like the worm he was, too much of a coward to come after me, not enough of a man to make it right.

It was the first and only time I asked my parents to intervene in one of my relationships and I felt a little dishonest about doing it that way, but OH how I loved the quick clean kill that chopped Paul out of my life. Boom. Just like that. My FREEDOM, instantly granted! Why couldn't it always be that way?

ೲ Form Follows Function ೫

⌘

By age seventeen, I couldn't ignore that I was getting increasingly nervous, moody, and fearful. I couldn't get comfortable anyplace, not even in bed. My legs were too restless. My breasts were too sensitive. My mind raced. I felt a growing cognitive dissonance with my surroundings. The world was an angry, hostile place.

Everywhere I roamed, I was on guard against junkies, con artists, drunks, thieves, and garden-variety perverts who wanted to mess with my head. Their unkindness disturbed me. Their interpersonal violence and lack of self-respect repulsed me. But it was the world I was born to navigate, so I resolved to steer through it at maximum velocity. Side-stepping danger became my art as I zigzagged around the sleaze and avoided confrontations.

When I was fourteen, I got flashed by a creepy guy at the Church Avenue Station. It was my first encounter with deliberate public sex. He was an ugly putz who popped open his raincoat and waggled his small dick at me. I wasn't so much shocked as flustered that he looked exactly like a flasher in a cartoon, as if he'd learned the technique from *MAD* magazine. When my friends caught up to me, they wanted us to hunt him down and gang up on him, Brooklyn-style. I didn't see the point. We weren't the sex police. We were hippies.

You don't grow up in a rough neighborhood without your share of close encounters. Besides, petty criminals were part of the urban landscape, as common as cockroaches. The city was their spawning ground. They lurked in doorways and slipped anonymously through crowds, using the subway system as toilets so the stench of their nihilism followed you through the tunnels and into the streets. From my Holocaustic point of view, the stink reminded you of the reality of life.

I got used to the idea that you were never really in control in the city. Sudden catastrophe could drop from a window and land on your head, or it could spring from a shadow and press a knife to your throat. I got mugged on my way to music school by a gang of girls, pick-pocketed outside Trinity Church on Wall Street, and sexually accosted almost every day I was out on my own. Men had no reservations about catcalling or shouting obscenities or sidling up to you and trying to cop a feel. Rush hour on the subway was like full-body rape. I once rode a man's stiff erection from DeKalb Avenue to 34th Street, helplessly wedged in a twerk. We each tried to move but it only made things worse. I couldn't blame his dick, and he couldn't blame my ass, so we just endured in silence until the doors opened at my stop, without ever making eye contact.

It was New York, the greatest city in the world. Madness was the mystery sauce in its melting pot – one taste woke you up to the reality of 8 million frogs in a concrete pond. Shit happened in New York that could not be explained in ways people who weren't from the city would understand.

So the fuck what, I told myself as I darted past miscreants and creepazoids who flicked their tongues at me. Not random molestations nor exposed dicks, not the junkies who always looked like they were ready to kill you if they could only walk straight, not the specter of imminent death could slow me down. I couldn't slow down. There was nothing to slow down for. I was raised in the gutters, there was nowhere else to look but the skies. I took my moral instructions from poets! From William

Blake, who said that "the road of excess leads to the palace of wisdom" and "sooner murder an infant in its cradle than nurse unacted desires." I worshiped Oscar Wilde's words,

"Never regret thy fall,
O Icarus of the fearless flight
For the greatest tragedy of them all
Is never to feel the burning light."

Manhattan was my burning light. I flew to it. I had to. It felt like salvation. It wasn't New York life that stressed me out. I stressed me out. Me. I could not get my shit together. No matter what I did, I was never good enough. I was a competent pianist, but not gifted. My school grades were good but not great. Teachers constantly asked me, "Why aren't you doing better?" I didn't know. Why should I do better? What did they expect of me? When it interested me, I devoured it. When it bored me, I drew unflattering cartoons of the teachers and passed them around to friends. I wanted to fly through life at the speed of light, not feel burdened by the tedium of being trapped in a room answering irrelevant questions.

Practicing to become something, studying for hours so I could get a boring job at some future date, those things were not for me. I was on fire, from my toes to my brain down into my soul, ready to explode. I wanted life experience. I wanted love. Random, carefree, no-strings love that was nonetheless meaningful and deep. I wanted a life without moronic conversations and fights with my mother. I wanted to own more books, and I wanted to travel abroad, and I wanted a pair of really cool jeans, the kind that rich hippies and rock stars wore that hugged their asses just right. I didn't want my life in Brooklyn. I'd rather sleep in a rat-infested basement with someone who really loved me than in my parents' home. I could do it. I could rationalize anything for the sake of love.

I was the most courageous person I knew and the most cowardly, the most aggressive and the shyest. I watched myself go through the motions of life with cool detachment, while hypochondria made me secretly check my pulse and feel my forehead every hour. When no one was around, I panicked and cried and stayed up all night watching television, and at the same time, I judged myself and loathed my weakness. Survive a Holocaust? I couldn't even go 20 minutes without thinking I was dying.

I had to push harder, further, deeper or I'd never survive real life, real, hard, scary life. I stayed up later than other people, I ate less than other people, I had more sex than other people, I wrote more, I worried more, I thought more, I questioned more, and the more I wanted, the more I forced myself to pretend to be brave.

I'd ride between subway cars when the train passed over the Manhattan Bridge, challenging myself to look down between the jolting cars, through the webs of tracks and girders to the rushing green waters of the East River. I was terrified of heights, of falling, of drowning, but I willed myself to look anyway. I'd spread my legs and planted a foot on each platform, then waited to be frightened when the train swayed and jolted, stretching me out like a wishbone and snapping me back together.

I was immortal then. I could go anywhere and do anything and live to write about it. I'd get off in Manhattan feeling revitalized, and wander and rove aimlessly until it was time to go home. Sometimes, I got off at 42nd Street to absorb the porn circus, checking out the hustlers and hookers, reading posters and lobby cards, watching the nude dancers from the doorway of the Metro Club on Broadway. I dawdled outside gay movie theaters on 8th Avenue where windowless walls and censored lobby cards left so much to the imagination. Once, I lied about my age and got into the World Theatre to see *Deep Throat*. As I watched from a front row seat, I heard strange whooshing sounds behind me. I turned and made out several stony-faced men, eyes glued to the screen, seated far apart from one another. Their raincoats rustling like petticoats as they massaged their dicks. I wondered what would happen if I asked one if he'd like a hand, but it was creepy and sad, not unlike the movie I was watching, which made sex look so ridiculous and enjoyable only to really dumb people.

No matter the shabbiness, the silliness, it was raw and real. If it was sleazy, well, so was life. I could see myself as the madam of a high-priced establishment that catered to every taste. I could imagine letting someone rent my sexual charms as long as he understood he could never own me. Being a porn actress would be an amazing experience, I thought, so radical, so different, so adventurous. And then there were all those hot male porn stars with their legendary penises!

But first, I had to get out of my parents' house. I knew since I was ten that I had to get away but now, in my teens, the practical impossibility of it became a cross for my back. After getting an application from one place, I knew I was doomed. No employer, no references, no rental history and definitely not enough money to rent an apartment on my own. I needed a roommate but I couldn't imagine who would want me. All my friends lived at home or in college dorms, except for the one who went to India to join an ashram. I was not that desperate yet.

I decided to venture to Upper Broadway and a new hippie-style business, where ordinary people could barter goods and services. Their ads filled the back pages of *The Village Voice*, and read "Everything for Everybody: that is what we do." I hoped they'd do something for me, namely match me up with one of the sweet work-for-rent deals they heavily promoted in their ads. "Light housework in exchange for gorgeous room overlooking park" and "Light office work for free room in great neighborhood" sounded ideal to me.

When I got there, I eagerly scoured the metal boxes, arranged by category, which contained index cards listing the job and the contact. It was fantastic. Apparently, all over New York, people with too much space needed people to fill it in exchange for a few hours of typing or light tidying. That was a better deal than I had at home. I carefully copied the best three offers into my notebook.

The first place I went to was near Columbia University, and while the room was hideous, it was walking distance to used bookstores, cheap coffee shops and a nightlife. After telling me I was the first to see it, and promising it was mine, my contact called me a day later to say they chose a tall blond girl instead. She would get the much sought-after closet facing onto an air-shaft that they were calling a room.

"I'm really sorry," he said on the phone. "I liked you but my roommates out-voted me. They interviewed a tall blond girl. They said you're too ethnic looking."

"So... you are picking according to who you want to fuck more and you want a tall blonde?"

"Well, no, I mean, I can't say *that*. But, you know."

"But. You're black," I said.

"Well, yeah, but," he hemmed and hawed, "but it's what my roommates want, I'm sorry."

The second place was an elegant psychiatrist's office on the Upper East Side, with a nicely appointed private room that contained a daybed and a big comfy chair. The shrink was well-spoken and immaculately dressed, a rich professor at Hunter College, who used the office only a few hours a week to see private patients. He occasionally had to stay overnight, but it was rare, and there was a couch in his office he could use, he said. If I would type up his notes, we had a deal.

It was a long walk from shops and the subway, but it was spotless and in a chic neighborhood, so I said yes immediately. The next day, I packed some clothes and possessions in shopping bags and filled my knapsack with textbooks, sneaking it all out of my parents' house. I planned stealthily to transport my paltry belongings one shopping bag at a time, hoping my parents wouldn't notice until everything I needed was gone. I schlepped to the train with the bags, and made the slow and difficult journey up to my new place.

I let myself into the office with the key he gave me, and unpacked my books. It was magnificently silent and spotless. I had to hand in a paper the next day on Wordsworth's classic line that poetry is "emotion recollected in tranquility." So I got to work on his fancy Selectric – which I'd eyed gleefully during the interview – grooving on the solitude, and still typing after dark when the front door opened. In popped the psychiatrist, saying something came up at the last minute and he needed to spend the night there. I tried to stay focused as he hovered around me, impatient that he was urging me to finish up so he could get some sleep but afraid to piss him off, lest it kill the deal.

He was extremely short and thin, small boned and refined, as if his tiny white hands had never touched anything dirtier than his own starched underwear. I remember his build clearly because, as soon as the lights went off, he turned into a sex goblin.

He climbed on top of me. I pushed him off of me. He climbed back on. I pushed him back off. He grabbed my shoulders. I grabbed his neck. He tried to wrestle me into submission. I put a lock on him that made him screech. You couldn't tell, because I was so small, but I had muscles under my muscles, and years of rage under that. He wasn't the first male I'd wrestled off of me.

"I'm sorry, I'm sorry," he said after each defeat, running to the other room to lick his wounded ego.

Emboldened by my realization that I could beat the shit out of this cockroach of a man, I traipsed back and forth from the daybed to the analyst's couch to evade him, lying down fully dressed and clutching my purse, trying to get in a few winks between futile assaults.

Ten minutes, twenty minutes, however long it took him to succumb to his demons, he'd return and re-enact the psychotic sex comedy one more time. The more he aggravated me, the colder I felt inside.

I could not understand why he kept asking for more abuse but I didn't want to head into the New York night. The streets and subways weren't safe at 2 a.m. Even if I made it, I couldn't wake my parents up and get caught laden down like a bag lady. Plus my paper on tranquility was due at 9 a.m. in Queens and I had a major crush on the teacher, so handing it in late was not even an option. Had it been for physics or geology, fuck it, but this was Wordsworth.

It was safer to stick to the plan and wrestle than to flee and risk the streets. When he launched his next assault, I fought for real and accidentally threw him to the floor. He mumbled about his back and didn't return for half an hour. So the next time he crawled on me, I threw him to the floor with all the malice I could muster. He moaned and rolled around, caterwauling about his back, while I looked down from the analyst's couch and watched in stony silence. At last, he got to his feet and limped away, never to be seen again.

I jumped up at dawn, got all my stuff together, and slid the key under the door behind me. I dragged the bags with me to school and then back to my parents' house that evening without anyone ever knowing I'd almost moved out. I considered calling Hunter College to report him but, in the end, wasn't sure who they would believe: the ragged Brooklyn girl who beat him up or the rich psychiatrist who would undoubtedly claim I was a psychotic he kindly tried to save?

I brushed myself off and moved on to the next name on the list I'd made at Everything for Everybody. I saved it for last because the location was barely a mile from my parents' place. It wasn't Manhattan, but the building faced Sheepshead Bay, guaranteeing a beautiful view every day in a neighborhood I knew and loved. The landlord described himself as "elderly gentleman," and the card said he needed someone to help him keep his place in order. The idea of helping an old guy touched me. I never had a grandfather. I imagined a little old man welcoming me in and telling me all about his grandchildren, and me heating cans of soup for him on winter days.

When I got there, a fat man in a silk smoking jacket greeted me like a duchess, kissing my hands. The hair on his head was dyed jet-black but his mustache was so white I felt like dabbing a finger into the shoe polish on his head and touching up the stache so it matched. He gently pulled me through the doorway. Sensing my hesitation, he explained that he was Romanian, and that was how they greeted all beautiful women.

He ushered me through the narrow foyer to a living room piled floor to ceiling with theater memorabilia. Every inch of the walls were covered in framed black and whites of him mugging for the camera with minor celebrities. He pushed some stacks aside and invited me to sit on his plastic-covered sofa, then darted to an antique record player.

"You will love this!" he said, breathing hard as he carefully placed the needle over the record.

He played the "Flight of the Bumblebee" and, when it was done, he played it again, at some point picking up an invisible violin and air-fiddling with uncomfortably undistilled emotion and making self-satisfied grunts with every phrase. I didn't know what was going on and nodded my head with a vague smile. I tried to get a peek at the Bay outside but records and notebooks were stacked so high they blocked the view.

"I am an impresario!" he announced, plopping beside me on the couch and pulling thick photo albums off the floor for me to look at. "I could make you a star." He exhaled and I smelled garlic with a lemon zest.

"I'm starting college next fall, I don't have time for that."

He thought I was joking and patted me on the back, laughing.

"Here, look, look!" He threw open giant photo albums, with hundreds of photos of him smiling the same smile beside Borscht Belt acts. There were some genuine Hollywood stars too, including Jimmy Durante and a teenage Adrienne Barbeau. She wore a dress that left nothing to the breastly imagination, while the impresario hugged her like a chimp with abandonment issues. It seemed like all the men were beasts and all the women were beautiful. I didn't belong in that world.

"Her mother gave her to me when she was sixteen," he said in a reverential tone. "She told me, 'Make my daughter a star.'" He stared deep into my eyes as if he expected me to blow him then and there.

"Yeah, no, I don't think so," I said. He was scarier than the psychiatrist. "I'm not the star kind."

After listening to another playing of "The Bumblebee," turning down his offer of tea, and glancing at the bedroom he told me was mine, I told him I'd come back in my best lying voice, and walked to my parents' house in a dark humor. Light cleaning my ass. Work for rent was code for pussy for rent.

Was everyone corrupt? Surely, the perfect solution to my problems was in one of those boxes at Everything for Everybody. It was my only chance of early escape.

I went back one more time to glumly review the cards. There was nothing new since the last time, and the ones I rejected before were even worse this time around because now I could imagine the desperate horn dogs who probably wrote them. I noticed a hot older guy started hovering near me, and by the way he was moving things around and cleaning up, he seemed to be in charge. When the only other customer in the place left, he came over to the table where I was bent mournfully over the box.

"How's it going?" he said as he pointed at the cards.

"Not so good," I said. "Seems like... everything for everybody but me, to be honest."

He peered at the box's label.

"No money for rent?" he asked.

"Nope," I said.

"Have you ever considered going into porn?" he asked.

"What?" I had, in a way, but not in a real way, more as a *"gee, what if"* kind of way. But now that he brought it up. "Sort of," I said.

"I make porn movies," he said. "I could get you into the business. Come on, do a reading with me, let's see if you can act."

"Really?" I followed him into his office. He was good looking enough to be a porn actor, with a ponytail tied back and a great body, and the office was filled with porn posters, some displayed, some still in their cardboard tubes.

"Wow." I was impressed. I didn't recognize any of the titles but I'd seen posters like that hanging outside theaters in Times Square.

"Yeah, I worked on all of them, producing," he said, waving his hand at the posters. "I got a new script here." He handed me a typewritten, bound script and said, "You be 'Girl One' and I'll be the guy."

"Um, I'm not undressing for this..."

"No, no, this is just a reading, relax," he said. He sat in the room's only chair by a messy desk. "Sorry I don't have a chair for you. Sit on the floor."

I sank down and started reading with him. I started wondering what the fuck I was doing and why the fuck I was bothering. I couldn't believe the words coming out of my mouth. When we got to the lines where the characters disagree about something, the porn entrepreneur suddenly kicked my thigh.

"YO!" I jumped to my feet.

"What?" He looked surprised. "What happened? Sit down, and we'll pick up from there. I'm sorry, but I'm supposed to show anger."

I sat back down and we read the scene again. He kicked me again.

"You fucking kicked me again!" I got to my feet and grabbed my bag. "What's your fucking problem?"

"I did it lighter this time," he said. "It's in the script," he said. "Sit down."

"I don't see 'kick her' in the script," I said.

"It says get angry. I was showing I was angry. I didn't want to punch you in the face, right?" he said as if he deserved credit for that.

"Look," I said as I pulled my jacket on and dropped the script on his desk, "I can't be a porn actress."

"Don't say that."

"I can't."

"You could lose a few pounds." He looked sympathetic. "Maybe get a nose-job."

"What?"

"Your tits are nice," he said. "I can tell even through clothes."

I huffed my way out of there, blood boiling, but by the time I got to the street, I was wondering if I'd just missed the chance of a lifetime. Was it really more moral to parse poetry for pennies in academia than to reap the rewards of amazing sexual adventures in porn? No. On the other hand, the poetry world wasn't filled with pimps and con artists. Still, porn. Wow. What a wild life it would be, how much material I'd have to write about then! And Harry Reems. Oh my god.

Being a porn star was infinitely better than having an office job. I didn't like that way he pushed me around, though. I didn't know if he was a real person trying to tool me to the porn road or a sick fuck who got off on kicking naïve women who came to his office.

I couldn't be a porn star. Who was I kidding? I could not do the one thing you needed to do to be part of that world. Fucking was still the key to the magic adult kingdom. I could not fuck. Could not, would not, didn't even want to try again. A little grinding, some finger-fucking, anything weird or different, blowjobs, handjobs, kissing, I was game any time. I even liked to watch men jerk themselves off. But I was terrified of going through the pain I felt the first and only time I had fucked.

Sex wasn't about fucking. Sex was about orgasm. Fuck the fuckers. Orgasm is what counts and I didn't need a man for that. I owned the secret key to me and I had no intention of relinquishing it to anyone else, or sharing it in a movie, either.

Sex was better than relationships. Relationships were too complicated. The worst of them gave me stomachaches and headaches, and the best of them made me lust so obsessively, I thought I was going crazy because I Just-Could-Not-Stop-Fantasizing-About-Him (whoever he was at the moment).

Even then, I preferred to masturbate because men were complicated too. I couldn't tell any of my lovers what REALLY turned me on. Their way, the "normal way," was filled with rituals and expectations and living up to an image of what nice Jewish girls are like, while everyone around you offered advice you didn't ask for. Meanwhile, I was sure that my fantasies would send them running and screaming, or make them turn on me like I was the freak that I secretly knew I was.

Too Much Pressure. I was happy by myself under my blanket with a vibrator, nurturing bizarre captivity and humiliation and power fantasies which gave me amazing orgasms, much more powerful than anything I experienced with men.

Sooner or later, I'd get around to fucking. It was inevitable. Everyone fucked. There was no way out of it unless I became a nun. A masturbating nun. But "inevitable" meant "someday, not now." And "someday" meant the unquantifiable amount of time it would take for me to deal with my fear of the pain. That turned out to be three years, and during that time I deftly avoided fuckers.

With one memorable exception. I met Larry in yet another hippie-pad-cum-parents'-basement in Sheepshead Bay that was a known hangout in my circle of friends. People were always dropping in and getting high, so you never knew who you'd bump into. I always saw Larry there, sitting in a big chair to the side of the main action, helping himself to whatever dope was on the table, constantly sucking on a bong he kept to himself, which seemed selfish, barely talking. When people got the munchies and sent raids to the kitchen upstairs, Larry would ask them to bring him stuff back. When boys called out for pizza delivery, he never opened his wallet. I thought he was the world's worst schnorrer until it finally dawned on me that it was his place.

After that, my feelings for him changed. I saw him now as reserved, self-confident, and generous. He wasn't a lazy-ass moocher: he was a lion king in his den. He was handsome in a brutish, big-nosed way, over six feet tall, with wide shoulders and big feet and thick dark hair fluffing out of his shirts. I began doing that thing with my eyes that I knew turned men on. I'd stare at them until they felt my eyes on them, then I'd lock eyes with them and smile, and then I'd look away shyly.

Eye-signaling was strangely meaningful to the male of the species. If they didn't come up to me right away, I'd repeat it until they did. They almost always did. It was like I could will men to me!

So I did it a few times with Larry, and waited to see if he'd bite. When I passed his chair on the way to the bathroom one afternoon, he grabbed my hand and I leaned my breasts near his face in that faux-casual way girls have.

"Why don't you come visit me in the evening some time?" he whispered. "I want to be with you. Alone. Will you come?"

"Sure," I whispered, "I'd love to."

He closed his eyes and exhaled a cloud of smoke. "Far out," he said.

I was so pleased with myself, I decided to go back that same night and jump on that iron while it was hot. It was such a perfect set-up: a handsome, laidback, dope-smoking hippie with his own private den a quick walk from home. I could escape there any time of day or night.

When he offered me hits from his precious bong, I knew I was in. He read a passage from a Thomas Pynchon novel, and said I should read it too so we could discuss the symbolism. When he got to "I had nowhere to go so I spent the day yo-yo'ing," I was ready. The book banter made my pussy throb and Larry's jeans were bulging too.

I lightly touched his arm and he looked like he was going to faint.

"Do you wanna yo-yo with me?" I purred.

He stared into my eyes so hard his eyes were like spotlights searching my soul.

"Gloria, Gloria, Gloria!" he whimpered like his heart was breaking.

"Uh. Yes?" I froze, unsure where he was taking this.

"Gloria, Gloria, Gloria," he said softly. "Oh, Gloria."

Then he pinned me beneath him and started grinding.

"Gloria, Gloria, Gloria," he murmured into my neck, as I struggled to get comfortable under his massive male body. His passion was as thrilling as it was mystifying. I didn't know if he'd been lusting after me for months or whether he just lost his mind whenever he got aroused. Either way, it was HOT, and when he fumbled for my jeans, I shimmied out of them without ungluing my lips from his.

"Oh Gloria, Gloria, Gloria, Gloria." He pulled down my panties. He touched my cunt like it was a sacred relic. "I need to be inside you. I need you, Gloria."

Oh shit, I thought, he's going there. He's really going there. Shit, shit, shit.

Sweat poured off his forehead. He looked so beautiful, so hungry, so sexually demented that, in that moment, I thought rejection would destroy him and forever define me as a prude. There was no elegant way to avoid the inevitable.

"OK," I said. I spread my legs apart and held my breath.

"Oh my God, oh my God, oh my GOD," he said, repeating my name several times more, grabbing me even tighter, covering my face with kisses.

The bulge in his jeans was massive as we tongue-kissed and writhed in a wet hot tangle of lust. He struggled to open his fly, but he was so hard it took several frustrating minutes to free himself, and then he realized he couldn't pull his jeans off because he was still in his boots, and they were hell to remove.

So, lightly bound by his own jeans, he started thrusting anyway while I waited for disaster. As I feared, he wasn't going in. Any second he'd tell me something was wrong with my pussy. He thrust again. I could barely feel him. At least it didn't hurt but I was dreading his reaction. Would he be gentle and understanding and help me overcome my horrible handicap, or would he be an asshole and hold me in contempt for the concrete vault between my legs? Either way, I was dead.

"Fuck, fuck, fuck," he murmured.

I blushed. He wouldn't make eye contact. He hated me!

Then I saw the problem: his penis was not living up to the promise his Glorias had implied. The massive tool that jabbed me through his jeans had withered to a mushy nubbin.

He spoke the seven immortal words of man: "This has never happened to me before."

"It's okay. Really," I assured him. "I don't mind."

He looked at me in horror.

"No," he said, "I'm going to try again," and began once more to pound the flabby meat of his loins against the dehydrating fruits of my own. It felt strange, like a bag of jelly softly slapping me between the legs. Strangely interesting. I wondered if I could come that way, but he was on the verge of tears.

"Let's not do this anymore," I finally said after his third failed attempt. I was feeling really bad for him, and just wanted to go home so I could think about what just happened.

I walked home in a state of giddy confusion. I really liked him. His failure to erect didn't change my opinion of him one way or another. Dicks go up and down, anyone who spent enough time with men knew that. But it seemed like once he realized he wasn't going to fuck me, he lost all interest in me. He hurried me out the door. Maybe I should have helped him out, given him a blowjob to cheer him up. At the same time, I was guiltily gleeful that I'd dodged a bullet. If someone had to be humiliated, wasn't it better that it be the man and not me? Still, I should have told him I had my own problems with penetration. Maybe if I had a gaping hole he could have slid his soggy penis inside. I didn't have to leave him to question his manhood. If I was a good person, I would have told him.

My girlfriend Robyn saw it differently. "You can't break down the door to a fortress with a wet noodle," she snapped impatiently when I told her about the encounter, immediately taking my side, even though I didn't realize there were sides. "I can't believe he couldn't get it up, after he acted so passionate." She sounded disgusted.

I reminded myself that I wasn't normal and other people were. Robyn was normal, so what she felt was normal. Larry probably felt the same, because he was normal too. They both thought he was less of a man for losing his erection. Whereas to me, the best part was how much he seemed to love me, how much I excited him, at least for a few minutes. His limp dick just conveniently let me off the hook. It was actually a positive for me.

I didn't know if I should listen to the normal people. They were seriously crazy. I planned to stick with masturbation and stay sane.

๕ I Am A Feminist ๛

⌘

The 1970s was when the beautiful revolutionary dream of a freer, more open and truly peaceful society withered and died. Martin Luther King and Bobby Kennedy were dead, Eldridge Cleaver was in exile, then Abbie Hoffman went into hiding and Tom Hayden married Jane Fonda, meanwhile the Merry Pranksters went rural, the Yippies fell apart, and finally Steve Rubell opened a fucking discotheque. I gave up on the male-led movements and switched to reading feminist theory and supporting women's liberation.

It was comforting to see other women try to answer troubling questions about the inequities between men and women, and to raise new questions I'd never considered before. I skipped the parts where they seemed negative about sex, and focused on the basic message: women are not treated as equal to men. From that basic idea flowed thousands of behaviors, contracts, commitments and assumptions that both men and women blindly accepted. But what if women were equal to men, as I believed? Then you had to look at the whole world through a different lens, and ask why women are, for example, supposed to do the cooking and cleaning, and live as servants to men?

It was still the age of sexual liberation but very few people were liberated on the inside. A new breed of hippie had emerged, money hippies who wore designer peasant sandals they picked up at Macy's and purchased their dope by the ounce, not the dime. Straight men were gaming the perks of hippie life by exploiting free love and most straight women were going along with it, because their minds were still enslaved by the idea that a woman is nothing without a man.

On my first trip to an abortion clinic I realized how the system was still totally rigged against women. My girlfriend was a nice Italian girl named Carrie whose nice Jewish boyfriend had knocked her up, and she was petrified her strict Catholic parents would find out. She picked me as the "girlfriend most likely to understand" and naturally I did. We walked to the edge of the neighborhood, and took a cab from there, so nobody would know where we were going.

Inside the abortion clinic, the pale-vomit green walls made everyone look like ghouls. Orange and yellow Day-Glo plastic chairs, set in rows, were occupied by glum women in various stages of anxiety or grief, either waiting to take pregnancy tests, waiting for the results or waiting for their scheduled abortions. Many of them had brought girlfriends to sit with them. I didn't see a single man in that waiting room.

When Carrie had worriedly called me that day to ask if I'd go with her, it didn't even occur to me to ask why her boyfriend wasn't taking her. There was an unspoken understanding in those days that babies and pregnancy were "wimmin" business, something apart from men, even the men who implanted the unwanted semen in the first place. I sat there stewing.

"Why didn't you use condoms?" I asked irritably. I'd gone to marches for abortion rights since I was fourteen but it galled me when educated women didn't bother taking the precautions to prevent one.

"He said they don't feel good," she said as if that was a perfectly legitimate reason for a girl to get knocked up and get a fetus vacuumed out of her. "He said I should ask them to give me the Pill."

"Fuck him," I blurted. "He's a prick for not being here with you." A flicker of hatred for the penised-ones fluttered through me. If two people fuck unprotected, why does only one of them bear the burden of dealing with the consequences?

"No, he isn't," she defended him. "I love him. He just... he just couldn't handle this. Besides, I think he'll ask me to marry him soon."

I doubted that a man who let his girlfriend go alone to an abortion clinic was ready to pop the question, but I didn't tell her that. To me, she was just having a fantasy with a happy ending, telling herself the story she needed to believe to get through a shitty experience. It wasn't my duty to shatter my friend's dreams. So I shut up and held her hand.

Marriage. What bullshit. If I was an atheist, then there was no God to give a shit whether you wore a ring. If I was a lefty, then I shouldn't give a shit about the antiquated institutions of government created to police morality. And since I was both, there was no justification for marriage, nothing that made sense, anyway, except mad, passionate, out of control love that made you know, deep inside, he was the only man for you and you craved to be bound to him and only him for the rest of your life.

Otherwise, it was bullshit. All made-up, cynical, sexist bullshit. Women were so focused on marriage, they couldn't see the truth before their eyes: men were trained to be assholes. They were taught they got free passes. They literally believed women were inferior to them, and that their needs mattered more and that they were braver and more intelligent. It was unfathomable yet it was how they acted. I'd seen revolutionaries still expect their girlfriends to make their sandwiches; I knew too many lefty men who let their girlfriends financially support them yet still expected the women to wash their floors. The worst were the men who lectured women on how to be a better feminist, even as they wanted you to suck their dicks without ever touching your pussy. As I saw it, what half of the men who spouted free love really meant was "free pussy and male privilege too!"

Sex with men was nothing and everything. Sex was a warm human connection, like telling your life story to a stranger on a train. In the moment, it felt significant, unique, deep. But real life was always waiting at the next stop.

In lust, I flew through a full range of relationship emotions in hours, starting with an interest that turned to fascination that turned to lust that turned to sex that then slowly drowned in boredom until there was nothing left, not a single emotion, just an urge to move on. When the "click" of sexual connection came, I was ready to throw myself into a mad passionate obsession without reservation. When the click turned off, I couldn't leave fast enough. Sometimes, I was done with a man by the time the sex was over.

I remember one boy I met just dawdling outside a friend's house. I never found out if he was there because he knew my friend or if he was just a random hunk passing through. The minute he started his patter, I knew he wasn't very bright, but he made up for that in cuteness. "Click." He had a relaxed and gentle attitude, which made him seem exotic, like he could be a California surfer or maybe even a Canadian. "Click, Click." He had a lanky, smooth, boyish body, a wispy blonde mustache, and stick-straight blond hair tied back in a ponytail. "CLICK!" I wanted to see him naked.

He said he had some pot at home, and invited me back to his place. We walked quickly to his meager flat in a dilapidated apartment house near Ocean Avenue. There was a mattress on the bare floor and one of the windows had wood boards nailed over it, but I didn't care. I just wanted to kiss him. We curled up together on the mattress on the floor and passed a thin joint as we rubbed our bodies together. I asked him to undress and touched his small red nipples and licked them, still in my bra and panties. I sucked his small cock while he writhed and moaned romantic things. He came. I didn't. I didn't even want him to try.

We hugged and smoked his cigarettes, and he relaxed and hugged me, telling me all about himself. It made me queasy. He wanted me to meet his sister, he wanted us to go away for a weekend. He was acting like this was the beginning of a serious relationship, not just a quick thrill on a late summer's afternoon. I got up from the bed, nodding vaguely at his pipedreams about our future together as I pulled my jeans back on. I was nearly at the front door when it finally registered to him that I was leaving.

"Wait a minute, I don't have your phone number," he said and came trotting out of the bedroom. He looked so vulnerable in his grotty little BVDs, a fresh boner hopefully blooming. "You're not leaving, are you?"

"Gotta get home in time for dinner." I slipped out the door, calling over my shoulder, "I've got your number." I lied. "I'll call you."

I walked home in the cool gray twilight, fully warmed inside, singing to myself, gulping the cold air as if it was water, drinking up the world as if it was new all over again, detouring past the handball courts to see if any interesting men were around.

I was on my own trip. My trip was love. In a way, I knew it was wrong to be so fickle but it didn't feel wrong. I knew my surfer boy would file me away under "crazy chick who showed up, smoked my pot, gave me head, and left," just as I've filed him under "random hunk I didn't even remember until I started writing this memoir." Love could last for an hour or five hours or forty-eight, and it could last for a lifetime too. I didn't have a preference, as long as it was wonderful while it lasted.

I wasn't looking for anonymous sex. It wasn't like any boy would do. What put me in the mood for sex with a partner was HIM. He had to be sexy in some way – a sexy voice or serious intelligence, a hairy chest or nice legs. The "Click" notified my pussy that he was worth pursuing, and the next step was figuring out how to get his naked body against my naked body. The bigger the click, the quicker I was ready to entwine him in passionate embrace and inhale his smell and get swept up in lust like a salmon swimming home.

Clicks were much rarer than real opportunities. I had suitors but none of them suited me. More often, it was a case of "he'll do" and not "oh what do we have here, oh my god." I tried rotating visits with them so I wouldn't have to spend too much time alone with any one of them, distributing my free evenings among a short list of boys. They weren't officially fuck buddies. Most nights, we just got high, talked about life or walked to Brennan & Carr on Nostrand Avenue for cheap greasy meat sandwiches that tasted great if you were stoned enough.

But sometimes, when the mood was right, or if there was a lull in the conversation, one of us groped the other and soon we were a busy bundle of agile limbs. It was so comforting to me, because I had an incredible appetite for affection. I couldn't stand not being hugged or kissed by a man for more than a few days at a time. I loved to be grabbed hard, to test my body's strength against theirs, to clench my hand over their dicks and hear them moan, to smell their sweat and feel completely encased and enveloped by their maleness. I was more at home in a man's arm than I was at home.

I had discovered by then that sometimes the people who didn't turn you on at first turned out to be much better in bed than the pretty boys you pined for. Sometimes they surprised you with an easy attitude or cunning technique, and when that happened, their cuteness increased in direct proportion to their ability to turn you on.

Like my friend Darren, a musician. We had deep conversations that made me see past his skin rashes, his white socks and plaid shorts, and notice that his calves were muscular and his lashes were long. He was sweet in bed, kissable and sensual. I could feel the beginning of a click growing when we tongue-kissed. He was sexy undressed, with soft brown curls on his chest and powerful legs. Unfortunately, he couldn't keep his dick in my mouth during blowjobs, because when he got hot and sweaty, his eczema itched so bad that he scratched like a mangy dog. He started avoiding sex out of embarrassment and I started avoiding him.

There was my friend Bob, who smelled like Ivory Snow and had a slim, hairless, limber body. We hooked up at a friend's sleepover where everyone paired off in couples, and the sounds of sex were muffled by blankets. I got Bob. He was smoothly androgynous, and fun to cuddle but he never got hard with me so I drifted to his brother a few months later, a hairy intellectual who got hard when I looked at him a certain way. He was the least verbal person I'd ever met, and I was soon bored by my monologues.

There was my confidante, Chris, hairy and well-hung and great to hang out with, but one time he admitted that all he wanted out of life was a house with a white picket fence, so I kept him at arm's length and encouraged his hopeless crush on another girl. I was more relaxed with Tommy, a tall, shy easygoing guy from high school. Tommy permanently inhabited the friend-zone in his many female friends' lives. Mine too until one evening when we'd smoked a lot of pot and he was sitting really close to me and I suddenly decided that he was one of the nicest people I'd ever met and wondered if his long legs and big feet meant he had a big cock.

Our clothes were off a few minutes after that, and I guess it was my idea because Tommy was too polite to suggest it. He had a short stubby dick and a saggy ass, but when he lightly probed my pussy with his fingertips, I was dripping and writhing in seconds. To my amazement, he knew exactly how to make me cum. It wasn't a screaming orgasm but it was the first time a guy knew where to touch me and how to touch me and how to keep touching me until I squealed in joy.

I couldn't believe it, so of course, repeated the experiment with him a few more times, with similar success. He was really hot in bed! And nice. The next thing I had to process was that, despite our fun times in bed, and even though I really liked him as a person, the click was not there.

Yes, he gave me orgasms. But like all my paramours, he was too nice. And by nice, I meant boring. And by boring, I meant that he wasn't intellectually evolved. He bought into the idea of a black and white gender divide and ultimately longed for a traditional life with a traditional wife.

My father was the only real male feminist I knew. He thought women could do anything they wanted to do, and do it as well, if not better, than men. I thought so too. It never occurred to me that men were, or thought they were, smarter or better than women when I was a child. I learned that from the world. There was no way I was going to hitch my star to a philistine who expected me to launder his skid-marked shorts. I was so not falling for that shit. Unfortunately, there was no way of telling which man would turn out to be a flaming asshole.

I once attended a meeting of a radical vegetarian group at a rundown church in the Village. I thought they would be amusingly gentle people, sharing vegetarian recipes and planning community gardens, but the more they talked, the nastier they sounded. When one of them suggested planting bombs on sidewalks to "liberate" the soil so plants could grow, I got up to leave. I wasn't interested in that kind of revolution.

As I was going, someone handed me a sign-in sheet and claimed they needed my signature for their records. I hesitated before writing my contact information, wondering if it would show up in an FBI file some day. A few days later, the phone rang and when I answered, someone started breathing heavily.

He didn't say a word, he just breathed heavily. He kept calling back about once a week, until I got so annoyed one night, I yelled curses into the phone, even though my mother was standing next to me.

"Why did you use such dirty words!" she scowled.

"A salesman won't stop calling."

"Oh!" She was pacified. I knew she would relate to marketing call rage.

As for me, it was another set of data to justify my growing feeling that men were hopelessly awful human beings, permanently warped by social stupidity, whose penised bodies nonetheless held the secret to my happiness.

How I needed them. It was terrible how much I craved to be with them. It felt so unfeministic to need them as much as I did. It was like a mindless, driving force to keep an eye out for cute men, to begin primping when one appeared on the horizon and then to draw close to him. I was swept away by a tide of need more powerful than my will. It was as if a part of me could not be whole without a man, even though I grew quickly bored when I was with one. There was always another man – around the corner, down the street, in another part of town to be with, one who might be even more exciting.

Just as terrible was the notion that I had to pick one and vow to fuck him and him only for the rest of my life. That freaked me out. It was beyond my capacity. There were so many beautiful men, so many adventures in the world... and what if I made the wrong choice? What if I got bored with him? Or he couldn't make me cum? I didn't dare tell my girlfriends, all of whom expressed powerful desires for precisely that kind of relationship, but monogamy grossed me out. It just seemed like another con, another way to trap women and make them financially dependent on men.

I hated being female then. I hated everything about it, from the type of clothes I was supposed to wear to attract men, to the type of jobs that women were supposed to take that wouldn't threaten men. I hated that women had to wait for the men to "make the first move," that we were supposed to "let men be men" which, in reality translated to, "don't bitch when they fuck up."

I hated how women acted around men, too, especially in bars and at parties, where they transformed into prostitutes, accepting free drinks as their right. While I knew I had more sexual experience than most of the beautiful girls would ever have, at a club, I was the lonely wallflower in jeans and no make-up watching the parade of hair-sprayed, powdered, perfumed, and fake-eyelashed beauties charm swarms of eager suitors.

I felt doomed by my gender. Worse, I knew that when they got home and scrubbed off their make-up, they'd start waiting desperately by the phone just like me and millions of single women, yearning for a ring, a sound, a sign that somewhere, on the other side of that line, the man wanted to see you again.

It was a lifeline to the outside world, that call that could bring us news of a better life somewhere else, or at least a few hours of hot sex. According to all the advice, women had to wait until the man called, otherwise you looked needy and desperate, which would surely drive him away. So we all waited and waited, we women of yore, for eligible bachelors to give us a call.

Even when you had a relationship, there were ground rules women had to follow to make sure they didn't put too much pressure on the guy or make him feel boxed in. It was like men were precious commodities and it was your job as a woman not to drain them too quickly of their vital essence. At the same time, they had all the opportunities – they got better paying jobs, they got more social freedoms, they got taken seriously. All because they had dicks. It was all bullshit.

I never said these things out loud. I wanted to fit in somewhere. I wanted to pass for normal. It was easier to keep all the weirdness inside and pretend to be like everyone else as much as I could. So when a boy came along and wanted to call himself my boyfriend, I agreed. It didn't change my feelings for him; it just made fitting in easier, because I had a standard identity everyone could relate to.

I cycled through several relationships like that – with a boy I knew in high school and another I met in college and another who was a friend of a friend, and a few others I can't remember now. None of those relationships ever got deep or lasted more than a month, when the true boredom of the situation got to me, and I drifted away, leaving puzzled boyfriends behind. I wasn't puzzled: life was about forward motion for me. There was another man, a better man, a sexier man, around the next corner. I just had to keep walking.

I wanted passionate men who swept me off my feet, whose intimacy made me spill my guts and confess my inner thoughts, who made me cream at the first kiss. I'd had glimpses of such potential with some men. If there were glimpses with them, there had to be a complete vision with some special one out there. I couldn't stop until I found him.

My official boyfriend relationships were actually the least meaningful of all, probably because the boys saw me as "wife potential," and missed seeing the real me entirely. Not to mention that I thought there was something wrong with people who even wanted to marry me. Couldn't they tell how unfit I was for that role?

I couldn't be monogamous. I couldn't be a wife. I didn't want children. I wasn't built for that life. If anything, I wanted to be the opposite of the mothers I knew, the ones who floated through fogs of depression, bogged down by the tedium of lives that were chosen for them, not lives that they chose.

I would never get bogged down or be some man's slave. I had carte blanche to use my mind and body as I wanted to, when I wanted to. All I needed to survive was already inside of me. For companionship, I had magnificent daydreams. For physical pleasure, there was masturbation.

There was something realer out there, realer and deeper and more intense, and I knew it, just as I knew it was my destiny to seek it out. Whatever it took, I was going to find it. I was the Mistress of my own destiny. I was not like other people. I was free.

❦ Anywhere Out of My Life ❧

⌘

Every molecule of me was speeding through time. I couldn't grow up fast enough. I started escaping to Manhattan any time I had a few spare hours, riding the subway for an hour just to spend an hour in Greenwich village, just to fill my brain with new sights and new experiences, different air and radical people, and then riding home for an hour, making notes about what I'd seen or drifting into fantasies of what could have happened if I'd stayed.

New York was ugly to me. It looked ragged and filthy and mean. Yet it was the most beautiful place on earth. It was an enigma, a hell redeemed by exquisite beauty, and its greatest beauty was contained almost entirely within the sacred shores of Manhattan Island. When I discovered a hidden park, or turned onto a street lined with brownstones and trees, I was overjoyed. I'd find some steps to sit on or sink to the sidewalk to write about the peace I felt looking up at the fresh green fan-shaped leaves of a ginkgo tree or stumbling across a cobble-stoned street smoothed by the steps of a million ancient feet.

I never felt lonely when I wandered alone through New York. New York meant more to me than men. It gave me everything I needed to be happy. I wanted to explore every neighborhood, every restaurant, every art gallery. If the city only had a cock, I would have sucked it. I searched for each fragment of beauty in the body of the city, to meditate on it and merge with it. Then I brought it home in my notebook.

That was the closest I came to pure happiness, just me and my notebook, transcending lower class reality and translating the overwhelming intensity of life into words. I was New York's unknown muse, its secret documentarian, its faceless urban warrior, moving like a secret agent through the landscape, unseen by all except random horny men who would appear and disappear throughout my voyages as captain of her own ship. I felt complete and enlightened down to my narcissistic bones, delighted with myself when I was alone. I felt like the freest woman alive then.

But sometimes the writing wasn't enough. Sometimes I roved, window shopping or museum hopping but secretly hoping to meet a man, wishing the love of my life would come rushing out of a doorway and bump into me. Sometimes I went home with a stranger, wondering if by the end of our experience I would be in love with him. I wanted to be in love. The closest I'd come thus far were sexual obsessions and crushes on teachers. I wanted real love, adult love, mutual love, passionate love, as intense as the kind in books and movies. For the chance of finding it, I was accepting all interviews for the position of Man of My Dreams, regardless of resume!

Once I ended up in an unfurnished fuck-pad above a storefront in the Bronx. It started out at a pub uptown where I stopped for coffee. A nondescript man sat down, uninvited, with a bright smile and I put my book down. He snuck me drinks and pretty soon, he started looking like the guy in the Winston cigarette ads, blond and rugged and all Robert Redford-hot. When I told him, he was ecstatic.

"Call me Winston," he begged, when I asked for his real name. "I love that you think I look like him. I'm going to make it my new name."

"I hope you taste better than a Winston," I said.

It all seemed so funny when we were drunk.

An hour later, it felt like we'd teleported to his dive. I have no memory of the ride, just that one minute we were under bright lights at a bar on the Upper East Side, and next we were getting out of a car and climbing the back stairs over a bodega in the South Bronx. Never mind that unknown people were fucking in another room and the female was screaming so loud I thought sidewalk pedestrians might call the cops. That was awkward but it wasn't a deal-breaker. Nor did the mattress on the floor bother me because, by then, it's what I'd come to expect of single men, that they liked being ground-level because they were less likely to knock over their beers and bongs and ashtrays when they jerked off.

It was after I gave him a blowjob that I finally got a good look at the room and got cold sober. He didn't live there. Nobody did. There was no furniture, just old soiled mattresses squeezed into the room. It was a dirty fuck pad, littered with torn condom wrappers, empty beer cans, crumpled paper towels, and cigarette butts stomped out on the floors.

Everything about the set-up seemed shady. It could be a gang hangout or a heroin den. How did Winston fit in? It could be a whorehouse. I fucking hated pimps: was he a procurer for someone named Big Daddy?

"Tell me your real name," I said.

"Nah, I like Winston," he grinned but there was no smile in his eyes.

I started hyperventilating. Withholding his real name meant only one thing: this was BULLSHIT. I didn't even know where in the South Bronx I was, or if there was a subway nearby. Meanwhile, it had turned pitch black outside.

"I need to go home," I said.

He nodded in agreement.

"I don't know where I am. Do you know the address of his place?"

He shook his head, then picked a half-empty beer can from the floor and started swigging it.

"Can you drive me back to the city?"

"Nah," he belched.

"Well someone's fucking driving me back because this is the middle of fucking Canada and I need to go home now, as in right now."

"I'm too tired," he waved his hands. "I'll get you cab fare."

He went into the other room and interrupted the fuckers. A thin naked man emerged, a slimy condom still hanging off his half-hard dick. He extracted some bills from the jeans he'd left hanging in the hall, and handed them to Winston. The man gave me a defiant look and I looked back coldly. I was dying of chagrin on the inside but I wasn't going to let them see it.

On one hand, I was proud of my sexual adventurism. I'd congratulate myself for not ending up as a crime statistic, for dodging that day's daily bullet. Men were fucking crazy. So alien. So attractive but so mentally unstable. And obviously I was a crazy magnet. Even worse, I was DRAWN to crazy. Why? Because I was crazy. Like Mom always said.

I was a crazy horny pipe-dreamer, and I made reckless, impulsive choices for which I had no one to blame but myself. I was, in other words, a poet. And I couldn't stop. If I stopped, I'd stop being a poet.

I remember this one guy, tall and bearded and crowned by a mane of thick brown hair. I never got his name. I spotted him at another anti-war rally in Central Park, dressed like a holy man in flowing white clothes, his eyes scanning the crowd with burning intensity as if he was a prophet come to earth. I figured him for a Jesus Freak, or maybe one of those guys who believed that mood rings were spiritual objects. I was not a fan of the Moses beard, but I'd never seen such a handsome Jesus-looking hippie before.

Then he noticed me staring and came over. I thought Jesus was much too beautiful to be interested in me, but he motioned me to a rock and passed me a joint when I sat down beside him. It tasted rank, like someone had dug it out of a swamp, but it got me high. I expected him to begin preaching but he was tight-lipped, as all Messiahs should be. He stared at the crowds and I stared with him, silently bonding with him over our personal visions of humanity unfolding, imagining the world through his spiritual eyes.

"Come home with me," he said. "I live just a few blocks away."

Jesus wanted to have sex with me! I froze, too overcome by lust to say no. The walk along Central Park West was erotic and romantic. His profile was magnificent. He had a long nose and a big dick sloshing around in his tie-waist pants. Just north of 105th Street, he stopped outside an abandoned brownstone with a "condemned" sign taped outside the doorway. The door itself was missing and rubble was strewn inside.

"This is it," he said.

"But that sign?" I said.

"No, no, don't worry, it's safe here, they just did that to keep us out."

Inside, the power was off, the staircase was falling apart and he explained how to climb the wooden steps without falling into the splintered gaps. He slowly guided me through the gloom until, at last, he lit a candle, and I saw the ubiquitous floor mattress. It was once a stately apartment with high ceilings and enormous windows facing onto Central Park. The thick drapes looked like they'd been there for fifty years. One hem was lifted to let some light in, and the underside of the cloth was bleached light yellow. A light dusting of plaster chips carpeted the floors and the walls were veined by water stains.

"Is it really safe here?" I was dubious but he looked even sexier by candlelight.

"We get robbed a lot, but there isn't much to steal. Don't worry, they only come in the middle of the night." He spoke to a distant point, then madly grabbed me up in his long, lean arms. His beard felt gossamer on my face as he dove tongue first into my mouth. His being smelled of dust and dirt and sweat and New York City itself. Our connection felt so powerful that, for a few seconds, I lost myself in him, writhing when his huge dick swelled against my belly.

But something about him was wrong. Just not right. It wasn't the poverty of his circumstances. Grunge wasn't necessarily a minus when it came to sex. It was the way he constantly stared over my shoulder. I couldn't tell if thugs were sneaking up on us. It was making me so paranoid, I started searching the shadows with him, wondering if we were about to be killed.

The joint we'd smoked was giving me a bad headache. Even if I didn't get stabbed by junkies, the floorboards groaned more than we did. The building could collapse at any moment. The lust drained out of me. My temples were throbbing and my legs were jittery, like they knew they needed to run.

I hated my cowardice. Real poets don't fear decay! Poets were born to make passionate love in crumbling ruins with strangers! I was being a shallow, bourgeois weenie.

Just then, a ray of sunlight fell across his beautiful face and I impulsively curled into him, tilting my lips up for a kiss. For the first time, I saw him smile. His teeth were a greasy brown-green color. A couple were missing.

"Gotta go," I said.

"You don't have to. You could..." He looked past me again, staring like a cat at invisible fairy shadows. "Stay," he said.

I ran out like the place was about to explode. I heard him calling from the vestibule, but I vaulted over the last crumbling steps and hit the sidewalk at a sprint. I didn't stop shaking until the subway car doors closed behind me. Then I pulled out my notebook and began scribbling:

"Why do I do these things, risk all that I am and everything I could become for a moment's pleasure? After pleasure comes despair, inevitable despair. Why do I think I'll ever find peace in a man's arms, when a man's arm are the unsafest harbor for a woman like me? P.S. And those teeth! Fuck, fuck, fuck."

ஐ Curiouser and Curiouser ൠ
and Chloe

⌘

Nothing that happened with men really mattered. Men were no Holocaust. I could survive them. So what if I went to a condemned building with a maniac with rotting teeth? For one bright shining moment on the rock in Central Park, Jesus looked like my personal savior, so handsome and well-hung. So he turned out to be a bump on the road to real love. So what?

When I found real love. IF I found real love. If such a thing even existed. But when I did, if I did, and if it was as I imagined, I would give myself to it with so full a heart that I would die for that love.

That was my consolation every time I slouched home, ashamed of myself yet giggling, fundamentally depressed yet curiously exhilarated. From my point of view, entertaining as it all was, overall it kind of sucked. Sex was nothing like what people thought it was. For one, most people never fucked. For another, nobody I sucked off loved me. Even worse, there was no one TO love. I would rather be madly insanely in love and not be loved in return than to go without the experience of true love.

I pined and crushed and obsessed over men constantly, soaring to peaks of passion in my masturbatory fantasies. In real life, I still hadn't found anyone I could stand for more than a week-end. I knew that a higher love meant I'd want to stay when it turned to shit too, and endure all challenges. I sought that love whose hand I'd tenderly hold at the hospital, knowing my life was so intertwined with his that any life without him was not worth living. What wouldn't I do for the one I loved? There was nothing I wouldn't do.

Exactly how I'd cope with sharing a toilet with him or talking to him every fucking day for the rest of my fucking life were details I didn't want to dwell on, because both prospects seemed stultifying.

Men filled in the time while I waited for a love miracle to occur. Besides, every new man was a universe of unanswered questions and unknown potentials. Any one of them might be The One. You couldn't know until you talked to them whether they were the one who had the key to the gate that let you onto the path to a happy new life. So, when I met someone who seemed to penetrate to my inner reality, someone sexy, someone different from the others, how could I not fling myself with abandon into the relationship in hopes that I could be on the road to discovering a new home, a new family, a new life?

By the summer of 1972, when I was turning seventeen, though, I was starting to think that there were just too many men in the world ever to commit to any one of them. It wasn't because I couldn't limit myself, it's just that there was such a profusion, it was impossible to sort them out or take them seriously, even when they acted serious.

Never mind the catcalls and whistles, the muscle cars that rolled up to ask if I wanted a lift, and forget the generic lustbots who suddenly materialized like there was a magnet in my ass. They were the wallpaper of urban life. Every Brooklyn girl knew how to deflect them with a swift but murderous side-glare.

The bigger problem was that the number of men hitting on me was growing incrementally while my appetite for them was unchanged. I didn't know how to deal with the new ratio. It wasn't my looks: I vanished in any crowd of ethnic girls. All my girlfriends were prettier than me. I wasn't sexy like the snobby girls who wore tight sweaters and lipsticks that matched their moods. I was a grungy hippie.

It was my tits. I just knew it. They were a curse on my life. So many of my girlfriends had perky tits, tits that didn't require massive brassieres with three hooks in the back and shoulder straps that left deep welts. My natural D-cups were, to me, unnatural monstrosities, insulting vestiges of the primal past. The only good purpose they had ever served was tit fucking boys so I could watch them shoot off right under my chin.

But no matter how much I tried to play them down with army shirts and chino pants, my tits drew men in like moths to a Mosquito-Deleto. It was like they invisibly leaked an intoxicating "fuck me" fume.

This mysterious animal magnetism led to situations where your only choice was to run or to suffer and doubt your own identity. Once, my parents took me out to a small Jewish dinner club to celebrate a piano recital I gave. I was still in my recital dress, and feeling self-conscious. The way dresses girdled the body made me feel awkward and insecure, as if I should act differently, and try to live up to the dress by pinning up my hair, wearing jewelry and trying to get into role as a young lady. I was somewhat relieved that the restaurant was half-deserted. As I sat down, I noticed a twenty-something guy in a yarmulke staring fixedly at my tits. I raised the menu and vanished behind it.

Moments later, he approached our table. My parents assumed he was the waiter, and started asking questions about the kischke. I held tight to my shield and pretended to be fascinated by chopped liver. He pulled out a chair and sat down familiarly, then proceeded to speak directly to my parents in Yiddish, using words and phrases I didn't understand.

"Oh, no, no, no," my mother said to him, at last, laughing politely, "we don't, we can't... we're too modern for that."

"Did you ever?!" my father said when he left. "What kind of a meshuganah does that?"

I put the menu down. "What did he want?"

My mother looked suspiciously at me and asked, "Do you know him?"

"Of course not. What did he say?"

"He wants to marry you," she said. "He tried to arrange a marriage with us."

"What?" I couldn't make a voice. "Are you kidding?"

She leaned in suspiciously, holding the frame of her glasses by the wing to scrutinize my face.

"What?" I felt guilty and ashamed. My secret was out: my fuck-me-fume had leaked in the presence of my parents. Now they knew.

"Why would he just come over like that... are you sure you didn't meet him before?"

"Ma, are you crazy?"

"I'm just saying. It's strange he should just come up to us like that."

"Right, Ma, I met him at shul."

My father laughed but she looked even more suspicious.

"We were there praying for better parents."

Finally, she smirked. "You think you're very clever, don't you?"

"That's what religion does to you!" my father announced, ending the conversation. "It makes you crazy!"

My parents soon forgot, but the episode bothered me for weeks. It felt like men wanted to crawl into my life and hijack my plans. They had agendas for me, they had expectations, they didn't care who I really was or what I really wanted. They saw me and they wanted to classify me and stick me in a box. Even when they listened patiently to my hopes and dreams, later I realized they believed my hopes and dreams meant nothing compared to their plans and expectations.

What they didn't know, what I never told anyone, was that I had a vision of my life. Not a vision where I saw things floating around or heard unseen voices or anything spiritualistic. It was a knowledge deep within that could not be defeated nor argued against, and I can't remember not feeling that I was fated for another life. I didn't belong where I was. The life I would have, someday, would be as far away from my childhood as Darfur was from L.A. That life involved men, in the sense that I couldn't imagine life without men in it; but it had nothing to do with men because they were neither the journey nor the point of the journey, just travel companions along the way.

I couldn't shake that Holocaust feeling. Everything was impermanent. The whole world was impermanence, illusions, delusions, and change. Nothing mattered today because it could all be gone tomorrow. At the same time, today was immeasurably precious precisely because it could all be gone tomorrow. And yet, tomorrows did come, one after another, and they added up in time. If I wanted to escape the world I was in, I had to plan for a tomorrow that technically might not come but required some planning in case it did, which it hopefully would. After all, in my heart I was counting on thousands of tomorrows ahead of me before I was dead.

So now I saw my path, and knew it was my only path, as I had no other great talents in life. I was going to fill my mind. People thought I knew a lot but I knew I knew shit. I was going to get all the education I could, not just from books but from life too. I was going to go to every school and read every book and meet every interesting person I could, and drink coffee with poets and attend art events and, step-by-step, find a life more suited to a radical like me. Maybe a commune. A commune in the woods with anarchists and artists, so remote my family would be afraid to visit. Or maybe a women's commune where we all devote ourselves to saving the planet or rescuing horses. Whatever it was, it would be as far away from this world as it could possibly be.

The first step, though, was moving out of the house. I was working every part-time job I could find in hopes of saving up enough for a rent deposit. It would take me another year, but by sophomore year, I'd be able to find something in Queens, where rent was cheap. Meanwhile, I had to find some solitude in my head. The multiplicity of part-time jobs had led to a multiplicity of affairs in rapid-fire succession.

At one musty office in a former factory building in Chelsea, I got a job selling office supplies by phone two evenings a week. Oliver, the man running the operation was the most uptight asshole I'd ever met, and his constant pucker of disapproval only reinforced the sphincterian atmosphere in the place. For him, selling discount pencils was either the meaning of life itself or a paranoid delusion he had cultivated into a business model. I slogged on, since the money was decent. Then one day, after I hit some kind of record by making three successful sales calls in a row, he called me into his office. I was expecting a nice commission on the sales. Instead, I got his life story.

Oliver was a former hippie freak who spent the 1960s tripping his ass off while driving Ken Kesey's infamous prankster bus. He claimed he was totally straight now. His hair was painfully short and he dressed more like Mr. Disco than Mr. Natural, but he had only traded up on his vices. Instead of pot and LSD, he did coke and Quaaludes all day long. He'd dropped so much acid that he talked like he was still tripping. I'd nod sympathetically, an old hand at pretending to be listening when I was really thinking about cock or a poem or anything that wasn't whatever the boring person was saying.

He was too twitchy to notice anything about me. He took my ability to sit still during his speeches as rapt fascination. It was what his narcissistic soul had been pining for. I'd barely get through the door at work before he was waving and summoning me into his office for lengthy conversations I cannot remember because I wasn't listening in the first place.

Soon it was impossible to make sales calls because he took up most of my time rambling on about his LSD escapades in disconnected sentences, stopping only to make the other salespeople feel like shit for not living up to the standard I never meant to set. The more I tried to deflect him, the harder he wooed me. One day, he gave me a small bag of ludes, which I gave to a friend who had given me lots of free pot over the years. The next week, it was a dressy purse which I quickly regifted to a friend going on vacation. The week after, a fancy suede pantsuit, the kind that sold at uptown stores. It was exactly my size, so I didn't know who I could give it to.

When I brought it home with me, my mother stopped me to inspect it. "Where did that come from?"

"My boss gave it to me."

"What! Just like that??" She was awed by the fabric. "Feel how soft! And such good seams. Darts too! It must be very expensive."

"I don't know why he gave it to me." I felt weirdly guilty now, and a little dirty about having agreed to take it home.

"He gave it to you for free?" she asked, adjusting her glasses to look at me.

"Yeah," I said, quickly hanging it at the back of my closet. "He was giving them out to everyone," I lied. "It was just... suede pants suit day at work. I think they fell off a truck."

"Oh!" my mother said, even more impressed now. "I wish I had a job like that."

Merchandise that "fell off trucks" was manna from heaven, that sweet trickle down of the ambrosia rich people sucked night and day.

I wasn't lying about that part, either. I knew Oliver had Mob connections because he once took me to the great pencil warehouse in the Bronx where muscle-bound guidos with guns strapped to their chests were treating bags of drugs like they were gummi bears. I tried to erase the address of that warehouse from my memory because it seemed like dangerous information to have. I grew up on the edge of Bay Ridge. I knew the two golden rules. Rule Number One: the Mafia didn't exist. Therefore when you saw Mob types doing Mob crimes, you weren't seeing what you thought you saw. Rule Number Two: Shut the fuck up. However, enjoying the bounty of Mob criminality without any of the risk was every poor Brooklynite's secret dream.

After that, Oliver upped the stakes and gave me a gold Dunhill lighter. Out of curiosity, I took a ride up to Rockefeller Center to visit the Dunhill store and find out what it was worth. The salesman froze when I pushed open the door and sashayed up to the counter in my platform sandals and short-shorts and tied-off army shirt. The place was like a mausoleum, a virtual temple of tobacco products, and its high priests wore shirts as white as their hands. The walls and floors were so thickly cushioned you couldn't hear yourself walk and there I was, a Brooklyn bumpkin clutching a king's prize. I squirmed, sensitive to every patronizing down-tilt of the salesman's nose as he answered my questions and then threw in a free courtesy cleaning of the lighter.

After that, I knew the job would never last. Whatever Oliver wanted to give me next time, I would not accept it. I could not. His gifts were off the hook. He had entered the transactional zone now and sooner or later, he'd want pussy as payback.

I went to work with a sense of dread and tried harder than ever to make sales, but I never could reproduce the magic of my trifecta. I was, in fact, having less success now than some of my co-workers. Oliver wasn't as anxious to talk to me either. I was almost regaining hope that I misinterpreted his interest in me when I arrived at the office one late afternoon to find a booze and drug-filled office party underway. He said it was his birthday, and had brought a case of champagne and bags of pills to the party. Then he announced we could have the rest of the shift off with pay, and insisted on driving the girls home, leaving me for last, since I was the furthest. We drank some more, and he sped around town until it was just the two of us.

"My place is just a few minutes away," he said. "I want you to see it."

With that, he hit the pedal and sped up the FDR, finally coming to a halt in front of a luxury tower.

"It's got a gorgeous view. Come on, you'll love it. Just a few minutes."

It seemed like the least I could do after accepting all those luxury items I'd never felt comfortable accepting. His place was like a fantasy bachelor pad. The bed took up almost the whole studio space and faced onto floor-to-ceiling windows and a gorgeous view of Manhattan. Thick, white down blankets cushioned his lush bed, and a bottle of champagne waited on the end table, like he'd planned this all out in advance.

There was no place else to sit but the bed, so I sighed and surrendered to the inevitable, sitting down and then laying back to enjoy its surreal softness.

He immediately disrobed. He was even skinnier without his clothes, and his stick legs were adorned by thin black socks. He was rambling a mile a minute while I was having second thoughts. Now that the buzz was fading, I had no idea why I came home with him. I knew what would happen if I came up to his place, didn't I? I glanced at the ceiling and saw myself staring grimly back in a huge mirror. I poured myself a full glass of champagne.

He got into bed still in his shorts and we kissed awkwardly. An energy suck-hole formed between us. He couldn't get it up and I was relieved. Saved again by the soddy penis!

Before I had time to assure him that it was okay, he was dialing a car service to carry me away. When I got back to the office the following week, I was no longer the official favorite, but just another incompetent employee, subject to his wrath. No more presents and, a week later, no more job either. He fired the whole office without warning and I never saw him again.

During tax season, I found part-time work with a tax accountant, typing up W-4's. After a few dull jobs, he sent me to an address on 42nd Street, in a building just around the corner from the notorious porn emporium called Show World. He'd warned me it would be different. When I got upstairs, I discovered why: it was all one building and I was typing up the W-2 forms for the peep-show girls and for the old Show World's main attraction, "chicks with dicks." Thrilling! I tried not to laugh as I typed drag names next to birth names. I also noticed that there were a small group of male employees who filed different tax forms under variations of their long Italian names, some of them familiar from crime stories in the *New York Post*. Everyone knew the Mob was all over porn, so I typed silently. This was the shit, man!

The best part was when they sent me down to their adult bookstore to cash my check because they ran out of cash upstairs. X-rated magazines shimmered under display lights, stacks upon stacks, arranged on tables and shelves and lined the walls. I slowly meandered past *Bouncing Boobs* and *Titty Boom-Boom*, glanced at *Big Ass* and *Ass Mania* and dozens of other asses, blushed when *Big Beaver* and *Bare Naked Snatch* came into lurid view, then turned left at the corner of *Horny Housewives* and *Suburban Sluts*.

I worried someone might see me but quickly realized the only people in there were even more scared of being seen: a handful of men, most in raincoats and hat brims tipped down to hide their eyes. I strode past them to the cashier, who peered at me as if E.T. had landed at his ticket booth. I pushed the check across the counter.

"They sent you here?" he snarled. "What are you, 14? What the fuck. Who sent you? Vito?"

We both knew the guy upstairs was named Vito, but I wasn't going to tell him anything I knew. The cashier could be testing me to see if I could be trusted. Or they could retaliate against Vito for sending a kid into the place. You never knew with the Mob. I shrugged.

"OK." He shook his head and pushed cash back at me. "Take it and don't come back, kid. Go home, go to school. What's wrong with you?" he yelled.

I laughed all the way home, exhilarated. Getting kicked out of an adult bookstore was the highlight of the week. I hoped the accountant would continue to send me to colorful places, where I got to peek inside of secret and unsavory worlds I didn't fully want to enter but definitely wanted to gawk at. If he sent me back to Show World, I was getting into the chicks with dicks show if it killed me.

Instead, as thanks for the good job I did for his porn clients, he invited me out to dinner. We had, by now, met a couple of times so he could teach me about tax forms and talked by phone about jobs, and had developed a nice vibe. He was gentle and kind, a little patronizing, handsome in a big, klutzy way, but he was also really old and so incredibly lonely that even his clothes looked like no one but him ever touched them. Dinner was poignant. I wondered how many dinners he had eaten alone.

Afterward, we made a quick stop at his office to pick up some tax forms he needed for home. Then we were on the industrial carpet in torrid embrace. Like that.

He'd said all the right things and he was so big and strong and had a truly massive hard-on. It was a good dinner. He was a good man. I tugged at his belt and started peeling his pants off. He stopped me long enough to confide that he'd once had an extraordinary experience when a prostitute massaged his prostate and made him come without ever once touching his dick.

Then the cleaning lady opened the door, and we hastily jumped to our feet, buttoning up as we ran out of the place in embarrassment. Then he drove me home, taking the long romantic route along the Belt Parkway and pulling into a quiet parking alcove with a perfect view of the Verrazano sparkling against a starless sky.

I was enjoying the view and wished he was young enough to have some pot on hand to enhance the tranquil beauty.

He stroked my hair. "So where are we going, Gloria?" he murmured.

"On the next date?"

"No, I mean as a couple. Have you thought about our future?"

He killed it for me right there. I couldn't work for him now. I couldn't even look at him. The only future I'd envisioned for us was some more crazy typing jobs, and maybe a meal or sex or both now and then. He was talking about forever! To keep working for him was leading him on and I couldn't do that to such a lonely man. Worse, I might find myself in a few years with my hand up his wrinkled old ass, wondering how my dreams went so wrong. I was cold when he called a few days later, and he let it go, never calling me again, neither for romance or work.

No matter what I did, no matter who I was with, no matter where I went, I wasn't going to stay with anyone. I wasn't made that way. Marriage had nothing to do with love. In the heat of lust, men would propose to a horse. It wasn't flattering that they proposed to me. It just spoke to their fundamental lack of self-control, which made the ones who fell in love too quickly with me seem unsavory and unstable.

Men were animals. I loved them. Every one of them was like a cave I had to explore but every time I did, I ended up coming out the other side, feeling just a little dirtier.

There was no ecstasy beyond that moment of nakedness. The most divine experiences were the moments leading up to nakedness. Everything else, EVERYTHING else that flowed from them, was either script or deception: either they were following somebody else's script for how life was supposed to work, or they were lying to me to get me to sleep with them. The only true joy I felt with them was during conquest. Otherwise, nothing that happened in bed with men could compare to what happened in my masturbatory fantasies. There was simply no way to reconcile the crazy, secret world of bondage and pain with my teenage relationships. I knew I couldn't actually DO any of those things in real life but I feared I'd never have orgasms without them.

I did most of my crying over the hopelessness of finding true love when I was sixteen. By eighteen, the tears had dried into a massive chip lodged firmly on my shoulder. Fuck the world. I was who I was, I saw most everything differently from everyone I ever met, and even if I played the roles people expected me to play, I would never lie to myself about what I really felt and knew. My inner life was my magic bag, filled with tricks to get me out of slippery situations, to dance above peril and unman all monsters. I was born to be alone. That was how I was made. It was okay. Too bad if men didn't see it that way.

And yet, as fucking was inevitable, so too was marriage. From my family's point of view, when adults ended up alone, it meant only one thing: they were defective human beings. "Growing up and getting married" was a unified concept to them. It was the Catch-22 of straight society to me. You couldn't call yourself a grown-up until you got married and you couldn't get married until you were grown-up.

I know that even though no one would marry me for the right reasons, many men would be willing to marry me for the wrong ones. That was some comfort, since it meant I didn't have to live as a freak if I didn't want to. But the question remained: wasn't the whole system a big heaping pile of bullshit, rigged against women, conceived by chauvinist pigs and executed by sheep?

The truth was relationships with men sucked the life out of me. The best ones were the worst: I'd get all caught up, forget everything and everyone else, and then a few weeks later, I'd wake up and wonder where the fuck my friends had gone and end up paying huge late fees on library books. Lust was a frantic passage through hell redeemed by glimpses of heaven. The men I wanted the most were the ones who didn't give me a second glance, the ones who chased tall cool blondes in pastel blouses, the ones who liked boys more than girls. From a distance, they seemed to hold the key to my salvation. Meanwhile, I just kept churning through encounters and brief hook-ups, continually inviting the weirdness into my life, like the time I found myself in a restaurant at a table with four male friends, all of whom I'd had sex with but none of whom knew the others had had sex with me.

My inability to maintain affection for anyone was becoming a troubling pattern, adding to my anxiety. How could I feel so in love in bed the night before then feel embarrassed even to be seen with him the next day? Fucking around seemed easier a couple of years ago. Now it left me even more confused, less sure of who I was or what I wanted and, worst of all, a few days or weeks or months behind on my own life plans.

Men were the ultimate distraction: from the minute I engaged with them, I was off and running chaotically in some new direction. Suddenly, I understood why people chose celibacy. It was easier. No ties, no complications, no awkward conversations, no risk of accidental weddings.

I was better off without them. They messed with my head and delayed my destiny. I had plenty to keep me occupied. For the first time in my life, I had plans, real plans, plans that would turn into reality, unlike the oceans of fantasies that never went anywhere. I had a mission now: finish growing up and get the fuck out of Brooklyn.

My parents were going away for the month of July, traveling to Israel, and leaving me completely on my own for the first time in my life. Then I was going to California for two weeks in August, as a combination early birthday and late graduation gift. In September, I was starting college as a music major. I had managed to get all the way through school without ever studying for an exam. What would happen if I applied myself? I decided to spend the summer practicing piano and reading up on music theory. I would be the best student they'd ever seen. I'd also lose weight, save money, find a place to live, and swear off any romantic entanglements of the penis kind.

I began leaving my bicycle in the garage, sticking close to home, spending more time alone in my room, reading and doing needlepoint projects to pass time. Eventually, I drifted back to Vaughn's out of sheer boredom. It was a sordid new world there. The orgies were over and free love had shriveled in their pants. The drug scene had gotten so heavy that no one was having sex anymore. Now, I walked into squabbles about who scored the smack last time, and who owed who money. The soft hippie glow was replaced by the harsh and selfish mentality of the drug addict.

I didn't care. It was still better than being with my parents. I adjusted to the sociopathy in seconds: now I could come and go whenever, not required even to talk to anyone if they were being assholes. No one was making sexual passes at me, so I could read my way through Vaughn's library, interrupted only by the passing of blunts and bongs.

One spot of sunshine was that Chloe was back in the picture. It was a year now since her split from Vaughn, and they were friends again (read *Naked Memory* for the full story of Vaughn and Chloe). She didn't come by often, just often enough to keep me coming back in case she was there. I hadn't forgotten the time I walked in on her and Vaughn fucking, and how she encouraged me to kiss her breasts. Now she was living in Midwood with someone I vaguely knew from Vaughn's extended circle of friends, a woman named Mona.

I felt a little jealous of this Mona from Midwood. She seemed like a stuck-up bitch. She thought I was too young to be hanging around with Vaughn's group, and barely talked to me. She had some kind of straight job, working on Wall Street, and showed up once in a hideous wool skirt suit. I wondered why the consummate flower child Chloe was living there. But I softened when I found out that Mona was letting her stay there free until Chloe found work and could pay her back. Then I envied them both: Mona for getting to be alone with Chloe every night and Chloe for finding someone to take her in until she got a job.

I was coming home from the library with my arms full of books the last week of June when I saw Chloe getting into a car outside Vaughn's.

My feet sped up and put me at her side in seconds. She was wearing a diaphanous white peasant blouse. You could almost see her nipples.

"Heyyyy," I slowed down, "Chloe, whatchoo doin'?"

"I'm going to Provincetown this weekend," she squealed. She hugged me so tight the hardcovers made dents in my chest. "We got a cabin right on the beach. It'll be beautiful."

"Far out." I saw it: Chloe on the beach in a bikini, turning brown as a berry as she played on white sands.

"You know, you could come with us!" She giggled, as if surprised by her own invitation, then getting excited by her own words. "Come with us! Yes! It would be so much fun. Will you come?"

"Just like that?" She had skin like ice cream, cool, soft and creamy. "Who's going?"

"Me, Mona and an old friend of mine named Lisa. You have to come. Really. We need you. We need one more girl to help pay for the cabin. Then it'll only be $45 each. Can you do it?"

The math said that was a semester's worth of subway tokens but my heart said go. I knew the chance invitation was to save them money, not because they really wanted me. But Chloe. She was as beautiful as when we first met two years earlier. Her dimples and giggles were crack. I didn't know if she was the sister I wished I had, the woman I wished I was, or the first girl I wanted to fuck. To find out, I had to go to Provincetown.

๛ Somewhere ๛
Beyond the Sea

⌘

You never fall in love when you want or expect to fall in love. You fall in love when love falls into you.

You wait for that moment your whole life and yet it still comes as a shock. "Hello? What the fuck? What's happening here?"

All of a sudden, there is hope. Hope of salvation or redemption, of ecstasy or tranquility, of high adventure or homey comfort. Hope of change that will show you new horizons. Hope that love will answer your every need. Hope was like heroin.

The trip to Provincetown turned out to be more difficult than any of us expected, with traffic and car problems and detours and delays. It was pitch black when we arrived at a bare and lonely bungalow on a deserted strand of beach along a highway miles from town. We fumbled in the darkness, then someone found the light switch. The blinding glare of a single bulb woke an air force of bugs. They flapped their wings en masse. We ran out shrieking. Then we fell onto the sand, the soft white sand that was like clouds on earth, with the waves breaking just yards from us and the sky gaping wide to show its spangled glories, and we laughed and laughed, screaming out "oh my gawd" and "holy shit" to the wind. We laughed until we couldn't even breathe, and then we went back in and unpacked.

The cabin was horrible. The location was terrible. Yet by the second day, every little thing made me giggle. I'd never guessed there was joy inside me but now it flowed from me, along with a general state of gladness and uplift I couldn't define.

Mona was a revelation. Hour by hour by hour, we had not stopped talking, laughing, and sharing looks with one another that were like two souls surprised to see themselves in the other one's eyes. Some kind of weird osmosis was occurring, as if some of her was being absorbed into me and vice versa. We didn't just laugh at the same things. We used the same language. We saw the truth in each other's eyes.

Her straight life, I learned, was a good job with the potential to be a great job, working in foreign exchange. I'd never met a woman who knew about banking and economics, or who used her brain to make a living. I was impressed. I got it. The suit was the uniform. Mona herself was the same as me. We shared one soul and that soul was strong. The sky was bluer, the sand was softer, and Mona's smile grew more brilliantly enchanting as the hot sun coaxed the Sephardic out of her genes.

Mona was the only other girl I ever met who liked sex as much as me, or at least who freely admitted that she did. We could talk about all the different dicks we'd known together and her stories were as good as mine, like the one about the handsome young lover she'd taken whose cock was so crooked he could barely get it in, so she ended up sleeping with his father, a wrinkled version of the one she really liked but who could fuck her well. Her complicated affairs and dysfunctional relationships, her bevy of lovers and one-night stands, were familiar, relatable, almost comforting. Mona was not living by anyone's script but her own. I loved that about her.

The biggest difference between us was that she still worried it meant she was a slut. I was over that. I didn't believe in the concept of slut. It was just a word used by people who thought sex was dirty. Mona was more conservative about sex in some ways – ultimately I knew she wanted to find a guy and get married. But she was too hedonistic to twiddle her thumbs until he came along. I felt like I knew her before I knew her.

Mona and I had long conversations about the meaning of life that weekend. I know we did but I can't remember a word we said. The weekend only comes back to me in images, snapshots of happiness. There were endless hours on the beach, and endless walks through the town, and endless browsing in candle shops and silversmiths. Everything that was endless always ended too soon, too.

One night, we tried to get into the big bar in town but I got turned away because I was still below legal age, 17 to my friends' 19. I offered to find something to do elsewhere while they went in, because I sensed they were restless to get laid. But Mona wouldn't hear of it. She would not abandon me. I, so long accustomed to wandering off alone and separating myself from crowds, hadn't considered it cruel. Mona did.

"I'm not leaving Glory alone," she said. "At night in a strange town! No way."

Right then, I felt something I'd never felt before: emotionally protected, like she really thought about what might be good for me. It lit a little flame inside me.

We wandered until we found the one bar that didn't have overbearing bullies at the front door and didn't ask me for ID when my friends ordered me drinks. It was a lesbian bar and it was perfect. I'd never been in a group of lesbians before and was amazed at how beautiful some of them were, with long blond hair and perfect tans, wearing make-up and perfume like straight girls. I felt almost butch in my black t-shirt and grotty jeans, smelling more like a gym than a vagina.

Now I could talk and dance and drink with Mona all night, and no man would come over to ruin our incredible rapport. And that's what we did, finding it impossible to hold back our secrets from one another, unable to stop laughing at each other's slightest jokes, dancing like lesbians together to slow songs. I drank in the friendship like it was healing water.

When Chloe and Lisa, feeling left out and bored, insisted we go home, we slowly danced out the door, still holding each other, and laughed, half-drunk, on the sidewalks of Provincetown, where the bar lights and stars and bright pavement was like a light-show for the soul.

I didn't know it yet, it would take time, but I was in love with Mona. Mona, my beautiful Jewess with thick shiny black hair and hips that could birth a new nation. Mona, who made me laugh, who sang songs with me, songs no one in the world but us seemed to know, Mona who threw her arms around me, Mona who made sure I had something to drink and stuck a couple of bucks in my pocket when she saw me hesitate outside a burger stand. Mona who wouldn't abandon me for the sake of her own pleasure. It was Mona, and Mona was my everything.

❧ Child of Anger ☙

⌘

The rest of the summer was a swirling blur marked by two epic events. Mona was already a fixture in my life. We didn't see each other much when we first returned from our vacation but we phoned each other to report on every new detail of our romantic lives. It required an awful lot of phoning, as I recall.

The first epic event was my parents' trip abroad to Israel. My mother had stocked the fridge, left me money for food, and said she trusted me. I knew what she really meant was that she wanted to go on this vacation and had decided not to think about me for two weeks. I was thrilled. I didn't want her thinking about me at all. By then, I knew that when she spent a lot of time thinking about me, she invariably came up with new reasons to criticize me.

After spending the first couple of days walking around the house naked in self-conscious delight, eating big boxes of Bugles and Screaming Yellow Zonkers, downing Drake's cakes with Coca-Cola, smoking pot in my parents' bed to watch movie after movie on their big TV, and rubbing my clit to a raw nub, I finally left the building, and wandered over to Vaughn's.

The usual mean crew was coming and going, and after an hour, I was bored with it. Vaughn asked why I was leaving so soon, so I said with my parents gone, I had to get home to cook my own dinner. I had decided it was time to eat real food after my sugar binge.

"Oh!" he said. "You're all alone in your house?"

"Yep. For two weeks."

"Cool! I'll come visit you tonight," he said.

Vaughn had never been to my house though we were only half a block apart. But sure enough, around 8 p.m., there was a commotion at my front door. Vaughn was there, and so were two of his crew. I let them in and they squeezed around my parents' dining table, unpacked the drugs, and the party commenced. That night, and for a week after that, the drug orgy moved to my parents' house. Not only was the dining room table perfect for sharing joints and bongs, but there were two bedrooms in the back for anyone who felt horny, and a stocked refrigerator conveniently located between both.

Since I was having an on-again, off-again blowjob type of relationship with one of the boys, I required first dibs on my parents' bedroom and let whoever do whatever they wished in my room, where my daybed was sturdy and almost impossible to stain, tear or otherwise damage during sex. My mother's bed was big and soft and girly, covered in layers of delicate sheets and silky bedcovers and frilly pillows, and to me, generally nauseating, which is why I pulled all that shit off and threw it on the floor. But boys always said, "Ooooh, how nice," so I would grudgingly replace it afterwards, because clearly it turned them on to think they were getting a bj from a fairy princess instead of the tough chick who slept next door on an imitation black leather daybed.

It seemed only fair that I return Vaughn's hospitality by playing hostess to the motley crew that now showed up every evening to do drugs, and have madly high conversations about all the things they would never do and all the people they would never meet. One particularly stoned night, this one guy couldn't stop obsessing over his rock idol, Mick Jagger. He'd do anything to prove his devotion to Mick Jagger. He'd suck Mick's cock if he wanted. He kept saying stuff like this until the other boys started leaving, one by one. I listened to his whole rap, though, trying to decide if he was coming out as gay or just really ripped. But he left without explaining and never came back again.

Meanwhile, it was starting to annoy me that people were now helping themselves to stuff out of the fridge, doing greater and greater amounts of drugs, and staying nearly until dawn every night. I found myself sleeping all day and just waking up in time to eat something, hit the grocery store for soda and snacks, and receive my drug guests.

It seemed ungrateful to bitch at them, considering that they brought all the drugs, and that Vaughn had hosted me scores of times. On the other hand, they were obnoxious. On the other hand, I was obnoxious. It was too many hands to deal with. I floated along, and bought extra soda.

After about a week, my presence wasn't even required. The drug party had a life of its own. One night, the group's most notorious junkie, a guy with tracks on his arms, showed up. He'd never come by before but I guess word had finally reached him that there was a full-service cafe open to druggies at my home. He had unpacked his works and was tying off his arm and injecting when I sat down.

I'd never seen anyone shoot drugs in person. Only in movies. It was interesting in a ghoulish way to watch him tie off and pump his hand to pop a vein. Suddenly I realized that all of this was happening in the dining room overlooking the street, with the room brightly lit and its windows and curtains spread wide on the hot July night.

Not only could we see the street below; the street below could see all of us. A passing cop car could see us. Nosy neighbors could report us. Holy fuck, the next door neighbor was a NY

City cop! Any minute now, I was going to get arrested along with these junkies for heroin possession.

I imagined my mother's trip-of-a-lifetime to Israel, where she and my father planned to search the records at Yad Vashem for relatives lost in the Holocaust, being interrupted by a phone call from a police officer telling her that her daughter was in jail for heroin possession and hosting sex orgies in her home.

YOU CANNOT DO THAT TO A HOLOCAUST SURVIVOR.

I didn't know if it would have killed my parents, but I feared it might.

"You guys are so fucking uncool! You can't shoot up in front of an open window!" I suddenly yelled at them. They were so surprised. "It's not right, I'm not getting busted for your habit. I can't deal with this, you've gotta go."

To my shock, they all stood up and filed out silently, looking embarrassed, as if their own mother had just ordered them to leave.

"We didn't mean to be assholes," Vaughn said on the way out, which was more of an apology than I ever expected from him.

A few days later, my parents returned to find the house just as they'd left it, with some extra cleaning thrown in out of sheer guilt.

"Did you even leave the house?" my mother asked. "It looks so clean."

"Not much," I said, "just stayed home and read, pretty much."

I had not, of course, even cracked a book in my library pile, which gave me another reason to put extra muscle into cleaning the bathroom, as if extra guilt could be alleviated by scrubbing the toilet bowl extra hard.

* * *

My planned graduation gift of a trip to California was more intense. I'd never flown and thus was completely shocked to discover that it scared the living shit out of me. I had no idea I was phobic until the phobia struck. Every single thing about it was so alienating, each little rattle and buzz made me hyperventilate and claw at my legs in certainty that we were all about to die.

The time in California, however, was the opposite. It had a quality I'd never known before: it was all nice. My hosts were the friends of my parents who'd visited us in New York when I was thirteen, and their son was the older boy who taught me to French kiss (again, as detailed in *Naked Memory*). Marek was now a college student, working very hard on his English skills and his future ambition to be a doctor. He was even more handsome than I remembered him and his parents were cultured, wonderful people. Their modest home was nice, they were nice, the atmosphere was nice.

Something civilized and clean had come into my life. There was no stress, no pressure, no harsh words, no anger. The worst thing that happened was the mom served me a Polish specialty. I gagged when I learned it was jellied pigs' feet, and then expected them to criticize me for my over-sensitivity. Instead, they laughed and removed the plate.

The absence of anger in the household had a strangely calming effect on me. Everything was gold and blue, and the air was as soft as the light. Marek and I traveled up and down the freeway, in and out of LA's famous places, through parks and gardens. He took me to all the beautiful places he knew. We moved quietly, in union, holding hands wherever we went and, at home, after his parents slept, we'd cuddle and kiss on the couch. It was exactly the life I might have picked for myself, with everyone polite and thoughtful and sweet, and no drama or dysfunction visible. It made Marek even more beautiful to me, and within days we were inseparable, and he was talking of the future and forever and marriage one day.

For the first time, it didn't sound awful, though it didn't sound realistic either. I would be going home to New York to start college, and he had college and medical school in California ahead of him. I wanted to believe it could happen, and when we kissed, we kissed seriously, as if every kiss was a commitment. I didn't feel a click with him, but his quiet intensity and earnest ambitions made me want to love him more than I did. With every passing day, his face grew more handsome to me: his perfect chin, his aquiline nose, his pale blue eyes. I loved to kiss that face. I hadn't smoked pot in weeks, and I didn't care; I was dressing conservatively and making more of an effort with my hair. When I saw an upgraded version of myself in a mirror one day, in a prim blouse with a lace collar and my wild curls held back tight by a barrette, I thought, *I can do this. I can be a normal girl.*

The trip back from California was shattering. There was the prospect of returning to a place where nothing felt kind or generous or sane, to live in a well of sorrow with people who could never be happy. There was an intense loneliness and longing for Marek, which had begun with tears and sobs long before we reached the airport to say our last goodbyes. And then there was the flight. Particularly rough skies that day in August when our plane kept hitting air pockets that sent the equipment plunging time and again, and then lifting and speeding as if no one was in the cockpit. At one really dramatic drop, a scream of surprise rose from the entire plane, and the captain came on to advise us to stay belted tight, because we were in for a difficult flight.

It was different from the fear I'd felt about individual people, the fear that someone might hurt me. It was more like my ancient fears about a whole world out of control, about utter chaos and an inability to direct my own fate because I was swept up in a catastrophe so much larger than myself that I was just a speck of dust in its path.

By the time I stepped off the plane, I felt like yet another iteration of myself. I greeted my parents somberly and emotionally exhausted. I tried to think of the future. I was going to college and would become a brilliant poet and pianist. I would marry Marek and move to California, his parents would become my parents and we would all be very close and loving. And, oh yeah, I'd never get on another fucking airplane again, so I'd probably have to move to California by car. All I had to do was endure home a little longer and rise above it all by devoting myself to study and my beautiful future with Marek.

My parents seemed really happy to see me at the airport, but by the time we reached a local diner for a late dinner, things quickly deteriorated. My mother was obsessed with my tan.

"Why are you so tan?" she kept asking

"California beaches and really hot sun," I explained.

She dismissed rationality as a lie.

"You never get so tan," she said. "I've been begging you for years to get tan." She seemed to think I'd gotten tan in California to spite her. Or perhaps she didn't want to think that I was able to thrive under another mother's care.

"Are you serious? I was just in California, for Christ's sake." The bizarre, accusatory fights were starting all over again. There was only so much madness I could stand. I had seen the light at the end of the tunnel.

"But you never get tan like this. What did you do different?"

I was close to snapping when my father interceded.

"Lola, stop being crazy, leave her alone already."

Then he caught my mother's murderous gaze and froze, as I froze, because we both knew what was coming. He'd opened the gates of hell by taking my side against hers.

Not another word was said until we got in the car. Then it was war, each of them accusing the other of being crazy and stupid and cursing in Polish, arguing louder and louder until my mother started shrieking and drowned my father out. I massaged my temples, which throbbed as they always did when my mother commenced a new drama.

I didn't know how I would get through another week of living at home, much less a year. It was hopeless. My mother was even unhappier than before her trip to Israel. Despite all the glowing words about the country and its people and the friends they saw, they had not found even a crumb of a trace of a shadow of any of their brothers and mothers and sisters and fathers at Yad Vashem.

"We didn't think we would," my father told me, shrugging. "After all these years."

"But we hoped. Someone, at least one person, we'd find," my mother said. "Other people did. I saw!" She pouted. "Other people found people. Why not us?"

"Oy, Lola," my father walked out of the room, distraught.

I'd barely noticed the shift in the atmosphere in the rush of preparing for my trip to California but it all caved in on me now. The failure to locate relatives reopened the old wounds. There were no joyful reunions for them in Israel. They really were sole survivors. As happy as they were that they had lived, on some level they were equally unhappy that they had survived because of the guilt and helpless rage it brought. That fucking Holocaust. It was still eating us alive.

Their fight escalated beyond all proportion. Suddenly, I was hurtled back through time to my childhood home and we were mourning the Holocaust all over again. My parents could not stop fighting over petty bullshit but what really made them fight was Hitler. He was the source of all their unhappiness. His evil could not be undone.

My future with Marek ended in the back seat of my father's Dodge as my parents raged on over nothing and nothingness. I evaluated facts through the darker, starker lens of experience. I was an idiot to think Marek was serious – he had not shed any tears when I left. There was no discussion of how we would do this, no practical plan. It was a pipedream. Besides, he didn't know the real me. I was play-acting at being a nice girl in California. If he knew my sex history, he'd be disgusted. How would I explain going home with Jesus the Squatter? Or tell him that junkies shot up in my dining room just a few weeks ago? I wasn't a nice girl. I'd never live in golden California. I was trapped in this ugly sham of a life. California was a dream, a vision, that's all. It was time to move on to the next dream, one in which I could be more like the real me.

I called Mona the minute I got home like a fish gasping for water.

She really missed me, she said. She couldn't believe how much she'd missed me, she said. Life was totally boring without me. She was dying to see me.

My heart beat so fast to hear her words. My soul drank it up. She soothed me. Her concern sheltered and fed me. To know that someone in the gritty here and now cared, really cared, for me brought me back to life.

"I love you," I said and she said the holy three words back and we said them back and forth a few more times, to prove to ourselves that it was real. So many men had said those words, and I had said them often myself, in the heat of passion. But this time, it meant something bigger to me. This time, it meant everything.

She couldn't wait to see me. She wanted to take me to a new deli that just opened, her treat. She was meeting friends for drinks tomorrow, did I want to come? There was a party Saturday night. Chloe was off with a boyfriend for a week or two. I could sleep over Saturday if I wanted, even longer.

"Come on Friday and stay till Sunday," she said. "Can you?"

I could. I would. I lived for it. Right then, she meant more to me than all my silly dreams. Fuck my parents. Fuck college. Fuck my life. Fuck everything. Mona was waiting, and Gloria was back in town.

❧ Platonic Love ❧

⌘

By the time college started, I'd whiled away the last few weeks of summer spending as much time as possible with Mona. Everything was wrong about my life, everything except Mona and the secret life we led together.

When I was away from her, I slept 12 and 14 hours a day, smoked as much pot as I could get, and felt sorry for myself. The more I pitied myself, the more I pitied myself. I'd light joints wet with my tears, then write poems and let a few tears fall onto the page, because it looked so romantic. And then I'd call Mona and we'd make plans to do fun things over the weekend.

The first weeks of college whirled by in the typical freshman anomie, as I repeatedly got lost looking for classrooms and discovered I'd made mistakes at registration that I was now stuck with all semester. I hadn't cracked open a book, or done any of the things I'd intended to do to prepare for the school year. The biggest mistake was picking music as my major. By the third week of music theory, I was ready to quit college altogether.

But I also made some good choices, among them a poetry class, where my years of being an avid consumer of obscure literature paid off and easily made me a star. By the next semester, I'd switched to English as a major and settled into the happy position of being one of a handful of promising students in the English department who got extra attention from the professors. My academic successes amazed me, but I still couldn't find time to study, and spent my long commutes trying to catch up. I spent nearly every weekend at Mona's house, and with the usual string of part-time jobs keeping me occupied otherwise, my life was moving at supersonic speed.

Meanwhile, college introduced me to a new universe of men, a world of intellectual men. I'd never sought out intelligence in men. It had never even occurred to me that, perhaps, I would be less likely to become bored if a man was intellectually entertaining. It was what had kept me glued to Paul long after the sex hit the rocks.

Though I was trying to stick with my plan of studying during the week and partying only on weekends, time and again, I'd end up cutting class to wander off with someone, get high, make out or more, and then drift home at some random point after we were done. If they were one of the older, more respectable men, the date might include a meal or drink instead of pot, and it was more likely to end with a kiss than a handjob.

It was the teachers I really wanted. It turned out that a lot of teachers wanted me too.

It started with a biology professor. I don't remember much except that he was very sweet and had a magnificent red beard. When we went to bed, I was enchanted to see that his powerful, stocky body was covered by a robe of thick curls. His cock was as stout as a can and as rigid. I loved his body but he was smitten and emotional. The second time we went to bed, only moments after murmuring how much he cared for me, he confessed he felt too guilty to go on.

"Oh no, nothing to be guilty about with me. I'm fine. And, don't worry, I'll never tell anyone," I reassured him.

"No, that's not it," he sighed tragically. "I'm married. I shouldn't be here."

I hadn't realized he was married. I didn't want anything to do with married men. They were tainted goods. I just nodded my head, agreeing with him that he was a lout to cheat on her, and handed him his clothes so he could get dressed and leave. After that, he avoided me.

The next professor taught marine biology. He was only interested in my mind. This really fascinated me. I wasn't attracted to him but I was attracted to how attracted he was to me without actually wanting a kiss from me, or anything else. He took me birding in Jamaica Bay and as we roved the trails, he shared his passion for ornithology. It was like California all over again, a moment of heaven. Heaven was something I was only going to glimpse from afar. It was not my destiny. And, indeed, our day together turned out to be a one-time event.

And so it went. Random dates with teachers and short-term relationships with boys. The problem with boys was that they were too sexually inexperienced for me. I longed to be with someone who had more experience, or at least enough experience to be uninhibited in bed.

I was walking up the stairs of Philosophy Hall one day.

I saw a man.

My heart stopped.

He was tall and broad-shouldered, with a thick red mustache and a mane of pale gray hair, so pale it was a bright silver. His eyes were cerulean blue. Maybe azure. They shone blue as if there were LED's implanted in the cornea. His spectacles magnified the effect. Everything about him was radiantly beautiful. If lighting had struck him in the ass he couldn't have been more explosive to my eyes. I leaned against the wall, hugging my books, and waited for him to pass me. As he did, the tweed sleeve of his jacket brushed my arm.

"Sorry," he murmured, gracefully shambling past. Even his gait was beautiful: big manly steps, fluid as an athlete.

It was an instant obsession. It was like I had no control. Every part of me wanted every part of him. Mainly I just wanted to stare at him for many hours and feel his arms around me. The craving to be in his arms was like a fever inside me, rising to pitches that made me stalk him as nonchalantly as I could. It didn't take long to find out that he was an English professor named Dane, very popular with students and known to be hip and super-intelligent. I began hanging around the English department's offices and took a job tutoring English so I could have an excuse to sit only a few yards from his office and spy on him when he worked at his desk.

I knew he wouldn't want me. He was too beautiful, too sophisticated, too successful to want me. He could have anyone. He wouldn't want me. But I could want him all that I wanted at a distance, so that's what I did. It would be impossible, grotesque, to confess my feelings. They seemed so disturbed, just as my inability to stop spying on him felt sick too. We'd never even talked, no more than a brief hello or nod of recognition, like people who see each other on the elevator at work every day. Yet I was sure he was the only man who could make me happy.

Though it was too late to get into his class that spring semester, I had lucked out by taking a class with someone who turned out to be part of his clique of hip, liberal academics. Raphael was tall, but not too tall, athletically built but not over-muscled. His complexion was gorgeous and he wore his curly Jewish hair in a mane, like Abbie Hoffman. He had a perennially bemused look on his face and I liked his smug arrogance and cynical humor about most things. He was 17 years older than me, divorced, and a sublimely robust male specimen of the free love generation. When I took his course in Existentialism I had no idea how existential it would turn out to be.

Since Raph's class was the last one of the day, and since I invariably had extra questions if the subject or the teacher really interested me, I made a habit of packing up slowly and hoping conversation would start. Raph soon noticed me, and after that, we started chatting regularly after class, and after that he mentioned he drove back to Manhattan, and after that he offered me a lift into the city, and after that I hung around in hopes of being offered a lift into the city, and after that, one afternoon as he was dropping me off at Rockefeller Center to catch my train back to Brooklyn, we smiled at each other and he kissed me passionately on the lips, so passionately that cars behind us started honking.

It wasn't that we got along famously. He found me callow and irritating, and I thought he was an unfeeling ass. But that kiss, wow. Nor do I know how or when it happened or how it was decided but a couple of weeks after the kiss, which we both solemnly agreed we would never repeat, I was in his bed, telling him my tragic tale of virginal pain, and then he was fucking me.

Well, it didn't happen that fast. It took a little time, but he seemed to like that it did. He was patient, sensual and prepared. The condoms were in a drawer by the bed, he was freshly showered and smelled like soap and tea, and when he pulled off his shirt and jeans, he was as beautiful as any man I'd ever seen. He looked like a professional baseball player in his prime, everything well-proportioned, even his ever-hard, shapely cock.

At first I tensed when his fingers slipped between my legs but his fingers were soft and skilled. My spring-operated thighs which had clamped shut so many times at the prospect of a clumsy lover hurting me, fell open, welcoming in oceans of pleasure as he softly stroked my labia and clit.

Then he was on top of me, and I twined my naked limbs around him, climbing him like a tree, writhing in his sweat and then, just like that, he slowly worked his penis against my hole. All of a sudden, I felt it push inside me.

"OW!" I squealed at the sharpness of it, the intensity, like a tiny stab into the inside of the inside of my soul.

"Owwww," I sighed as the pain yielded to a new, unfathomably delightful pleasure. He lodged deep, pumping gently, slowly moving his cock in and out, stroking every nerve in my body with each thrust. Primal sounds vibrated from my throat, sounds I'd never made before and through my fog, I was giddy with laughter at what an animal I'd become.

The train ride home after the first fuck I could barely stand still. My legs felt like rubber springs, as if I could vault the rest of the way home like a kangaroo, as if a fundamental energy had been released in my spine that gave me super-powers. I wondered if passengers could see it in my face that I'd been rescued, redeemed, and relieved of a burden that had plagued me since fourteen.

I was not broken! I just needed the right lover! Raphael was him. He hadn't just fucked me, he had fucked my humanity! I was fully free now! It was better than love! I wanted to fuck him eternally! Of course, I couldn't tell him what it meant to me. He had warned me he'd break things off if I got too serious. *No problemo*, I thought. *I could play it cool, especially for the sake of sex like this.* I didn't want it all to stop. Oh god no, it couldn't stop. I craved the magical, incredible whateverness that happened when his dick went in my cunt. I wanted him to fuck me to death. I wanted to fuck him until I went blind. I never wanted the lust to stop. There was no drug like lust.

On the wide sturdy bed pushed up against the thick walls of his apartment around the corner from the Museum of Natural History, with the history of the planet in our backyard, we fucked and fucked and I sucked his perfect cock until we were both worn out. He interspersed our marathon fucks with readings from Plato and Heidegger, feeding me salads he tossed with blue cheese and thick cheeseburgers he grilled in his tiny kitchen, constantly re-cuing the Grateful Dead on the stereo.

Once, I had to phone home to tell my mother I'd be home late. He handed me the receiver while he was still inside me, slowly fucking me through the entirety of my conversation, while I tried not to gasp into the phone.

He told me to call him Professor in bed, and I giggled to be his obedient student. I stood over him naked on the bed so he could stare up at my pussy as I taunted him, kneeling slowly to lower myself on his waiting hard cock.

Once he told me to call him Master and pretended I was his love slave. I blushed. How did he know my secret?? I couldn't tell him about my bondage fantasies, my weird fetishes! It didn't matter – just using the language of domination and submission made me shiver to my core.

"Yes, Master," I whispered, "I'll do whatever you want."

Everything was going perfectly until summer vacation when Raph announced he'd rented a small house in the Hamptons, and that I couldn't visit because he'd be socializing all summer with colleagues and wouldn't risk them seeing me at his place. Keeping our relationship secret was something I'd readily agreed to but now that I was being abandoned for three months, I saw it differently and understood it the way I understood things then: I was good enough to fuck in secret but not good enough for anyone to know he was fucking me. I was the dirty secret on the side.

I didn't cry about it. I didn't know what I felt. I didn't feel anything. What else did I expect? He wasn't really into me. I acted tough on the outside, capable of dealing with everything. Inside, though, were a million sharp jigsaw pieces and none of them fit.

"He's going away for the whole summer and won't see you?" Mona was angry for me. "What a prick! Fuck him," she said. "Besides, you have better things to do this summer."

"I do?" I was finding it hard to function just then. I couldn't stop sleeping. Even when I was awake, I felt asleep. I wasn't hungry or thirsty. When I went outside, the world looked so surreal, I hurried home again and turned on the TV to drown out the thoughts in my head.

"There will be more time for us," Mona said.

"Us." Two letters, one word, the return of hope. I had someone in my life, someone I could always count on. I had Mona. I didn't need a man, not when I had Mona. She was right. There were better things to do. There would be better men to fuck, too, ones I'd love and leave, knowing that the only true love was platonic love, the love I shared with Mona.

Mona was my comfort in life. We never fought. We barely disagreed about anything. That was the beauty of our friendship. We fit together easily and grew together naturally, flowing in harmony like conjoined streams. That is what I believed. One week we took a jewelry class together, another week we went to a tap-dancing class, and some Saturday nights we stayed at home, with a good movie on TV and cats in our laps. Sometimes we danced together in the living room or sang along to Joni Mitchell records. Sometimes we fell asleep together in her bed after talking all night. I'd wake up to find her curled up beside me and feel a sense of wholeness I'd never known before. Then I'd tiptoe barefoot to the bathroom, stepping carefully around the overflowing litterbox, parting the curtains of underwear hanging off the shower, to sit on the toilet and wonder how I could make this my life. I wished Chloe would move out so I could occupy the bed in the living room permanently.

The only thorn in my happiness was my mother. The closer I got to Mona, the meaner my mother got. Where she had never before seemed to care when I slept over at friends' homes, she grew fishy-eyed and tight-lipped when I mentioned Mona's name.

"Why does that Mona like you so much?" she asked me.

"We're best friends," I said.

"She's too old for you," my mother said. "What do you do when you're alone at her house? I don't want you spending so much time with her. It isn't healthy."

On and on she grumbled. If Mona canceled a date: "See? I told you she would want to be with friends her age." If Mona didn't answer the phone: "Call a better friend!"

What the fuck? She had never delved into my friendships with girls before. If anything, she had always pushed me to socialize more than I wanted to. She didn't even know Mona well enough to dislike her.

She wanted to stir up trouble, to turn me against Mona. Was it jealousy that I finally found someone who loved me as I was, someone I got along with better than I did with my own family, someone who made me happy? Did my friendship with Mona prove her wrong, that I wasn't someone who only her mother could love? Was that the threat, I wondered. Or did it bother her that Mona was a successful businesswoman who lived on her own, without a man, exactly the fate my mother was determined I would not have. My mother didn't want to see any woman, least of all her daughter, think that it was okay for a woman to live on her own. Mona was probably having sex in that apartment! Why else would she have moved out of her parents' house? It could only mean one thing: Mona was a tramp.

Between my talent for lying and her epic self-absorption, my mother never knew anything about my second life as a sexual wild-woman. It seemed as if she was only dimly aware that I spent virtually no time at home. As long as I dutifully reported in for dinner most nights, she could keep telling herself that lie for the rest of her life. In her mind, I was always there, being an obedient daughter. My father, who left for his factory job at 6 a.m. and returned at 6 p.m. never had a clue that I more or less kept his schedule, leaving as early as I could every day and not reappearing until it was time to set the table. Even when we were all at home, they lived in another reality. Neither of them had any inkling that I'd had successfully snuck men into my bedroom for hushed sex while they watched *Laugh-In* on the other side of the wall.

"Is she a lesbian?" my mother finally asked one day mid-summer after I'd spent a long weekend at Mona's house and came home looking cheerful and relaxed.

"Are you kidding me?" I was surprised that she went there. And even if Mona was a lesbian, did she think that would change anything for me?

I couldn't tell her that we'd spent the whole weekend fucking two Swedish businessmen, nor that it was one of the happiest weekends of my life because it was so free, so uninhibited, so random, and so filled with laughter.

The floodgates of fucking had opened for me and there was no turning back. With Raph's rejection stinging my ego, I now wanted to fuck as many new and different men as possible. The best way to get over a man was to fuck another one. There were miles of penises ahead of me. I wanted to work my way through all the races, religions, ages, and cock shapes and sizes. It would all be material for the book of my life I kept writing in my head.

As it happened, Mona had slept with a Swedish banker who'd come through town the year before. When he mentioned he was bringing a colleague along this time, Mona called me: would I like to spend a long weekend with them? She'd fuck Lars and I could be with his friend, Bengt.

His name delighted me. BENGT. "I want to bang a Bengt," I told her.

Even more so when we met. He was Scandinavian through and through, toweringly tall, lanky, hairless with a huge uncut dick and a mop of blonde hair that was so pale it could have blinded you in sunlight. So I banged Bengt like a lunatic. I knew how to fuck and it filled me with power to make him uncontrollably groan when I writhed. I didn't know what to do in the rest of my life, but I knew what do in bed.

As we were furiously fucking through our last night together, Bengt sat up with a surprised look on his face and began madly whacking my hair with a pillow. I had given myself completely to the sex, I was drugged with pleasure, so it took a moment to realize that my frizzy hair had caught fire from the candle on a shelf behind us and that my head was blowing up in flames. As soon as he extinguished my fro, I started laughing and rolled on top of him, pushing his cock into me, and fucking him like my whole body was on fire, listening as Mona's screams of ecstasy echoed from the other room.

I didn't know where anything was leading but I didn't care anymore. It was all about alleviating the pain, the anxiety, the fear, the uncertainty. It was all about fucking who I could, and getting high when I could, and drinking wine with my Mona, and sharing the dream that one day we'd be really happy. We had a vision of perfect platonic love. We made a solemn vow to each other. We would get married one day. We would marry each other and fuck our way through the male species for fun. Men could not break us apart. Men would never hurt us again. We had each other.

❧ I Always Expected ☙
the Holocaust

⌘

I started my sophomore year of college in 1973 in a state of emotional chaos unlike any I'd known before. I was waking up trembling in the morning, panicking on the subway for no reason, and by the time I got to classes, the world looked flat and supernaturally lit by a glow that heightened everything to grotesque proportions. The subways were dungeons of piss, swarming with predators. The sidewalks were broken and building facades were crumbling. I often scanned the rooftops in case of snipers. When I bumped into people I knew, they looked like caricatures of themselves, their flaws exaggerated, their pores enlarged, their hairlines greasy. And that was when I was straight.

It was as if I had put on the wrong pair of glasses in the morning and the whole day was a distorted, threatening blur. I was constantly listening for the sounds of rejection and criticism, always waiting for the looks of disapproval and disappointment. I couldn't look at myself in the mirror for fear of the ugly stranger who waited for me there. Sometimes I tried to modify her – taking tweezers to my eyebrows and plucking hairs until, once, I got so lost in the exercise, I plucked them completely and had to draw them on my forehead for the next two weeks. I compared myself to the models in magazines and felt like the homeliest person alive.

Raph was back but it was different now. I couldn't summon the same passion I'd felt only a few months earlier. Even as he seemed slightly more relaxed about being seen with me, I grew increasingly anxious just being with him. The sex was still fun, but we quarreled more, and he criticized me more, and I went back and forth in my mind about breaking it off with him. Just a few months before, it felt like more than I deserved to have him in my life. Now it felt like a punishment. He treated me the way I expected to be treated and I hated it as much as I hated myself for not deserving better.

Everything I really wanted, and the person I wanted to be, lived somewhere else, outside my body, in another life. The only gleam of hope in this one was Mona. No one but her could ever love me or understand me. I didn't know if that would be enough to sustain me through life, but it was all I had and it was better than being alone.

My first year's grades had been less than spectacular. I had spent most of the year in and out of torrid affairs, giving myself to weekends of pleasure at Mona's house, and sleeping 12 hours a night. I read every spare moment, books weighing down my bag wherever I went, but it wasn't enough to keep up with students who actually studied. Once again, I swore this would be the year I focused on my education but now I was finally in one of Dane's classes and he was more interesting than anything I could learn from a book.

I sat in a front row seat so I could continually examine his body, slyly scrutinizing him as I pretended to scribble important comments in my notebook. I paid such painfully intense attention to every word he uttered, every passage he read, that by the end of class I had more questions than any teacher could answer in an afternoon. When he read with feeling from the

Book of Job, "I alone am escaped to tell thee," I felt he could understand me.

I was so in love with him that I thought my heart would burst but there was nothing I could do about it, nothing, except try to be near him as often as I could so I could absorb him with every pore. His sonorous voice and educated cadences, his broad shoulders and shy smile, I drank him like ambrosia. I knew I would die if I never had him, even though I didn't know exactly what I wanted from him. I didn't want to marry him. I didn't want to live with him. It wasn't even lust: I never fantasized about him when I jerked off. I just could not stop thinking about him, day and night.

He noticed me and pretended not to notice me. He indulged me while pretending he wasn't. I was his best student but he seemed to think another one was better. Once, at a party, he signaled for me to come sit in his lap, then smirked to let me know it was just a joke. Sometimes, I lingered long enough after class that he'd invite me back to his office to continue the conversation or buy me a burger at the coffee shop around the corner from school, but later he would pass me on campus and barely nod. He did not offer me rides to the city, nor look for chances to be alone with me. He knew I had a crush on him; he didn't know what to do about it. He was kind and paternal about it, which made me feel even more hopeless. It was strictly a one-way obsession. I would die of love and he would never know how deeply I felt. Unless I died of madness first.

Something bigger, something darker, more troubling than Dane was going on in my life. The only time I felt completely alive was when I was all alone, lost in dreams about going to museums with Dane, and spending nights stargazing with him and discussing the meaning of life. I didn't want to leave my fantasy world. I was happy there, writing new scripts for my life and rehearsing dialogues of happiness.

One day, I woke up from the blur long enough to realize I'd lost ten pounds without trying and that my hands wouldn't stop shaking. As much as I'd talked to Mona, she couldn't understand. You had to be the child of Holocaust survivors to understand what it was like to have parents who were broken in ways that broke you too. Or maybe you had to be my mother's child to understand how deeply self-hatred goes.

Whatever was wrong with me, it was not the romantic madness of the heroines in the novels I cherished. It was not the zany charm of artists, nor the troubled genius of scientists, but the kind of nuts that makes you talk to yourself in public and which frightens children. The kind of nuts that, it seemed, I was doomed for, a kind that would get me institutionalized while my mother stood by, saying, "She's just acting nuts to spite me." The kind of nuts that comes from being infected by nuts in the cradle.

So I thumbed through the Yellow Pages and found Jewish Family Services, where poor people could get therapy for free. When I met with the newbie therapist they assigned me, she seemed so sweet and innocent, I couldn't tell her about my sex life. I was afraid it would corrupt her somehow.

"You'll need to bring your parents in," she suddenly announced on my second session. "Unless they attend some sessions, I can't keep seeing you."

I tried to warn her. It would be a disaster. She didn't believe me. She was firm.

"It's Agency policy. I can't see you again until they come with you."

The next week, I brought my parents. The week after, I showed up alone again.

"I'm so sorry," she said. "I realize now it was a mistake to include them."

It was small consolation after the event. My mother began yelling at me the moment I told her I was in therapy, and my father refused outright to go. They finally ceded as the date approached, especially when I told them the therapist was expecting to see them. The idea that someone in an official capacity of some kind, someone with education, expected them for an appointment was enough to scare them into dressing up as if they were going to a funeral, and drive me there in ominous silence.

The session went even worse than I'd expected, as I thought my parents would make some attempt to act as they usually did in public, which is to say, reasonably normal. But something about the closed door and knowing it was confidential opened a trapdoor into their psyche. Everything just fell out, mainly their rage and denial and unwillingness to hear anything from anyone that didn't affirm what they already believed.

"I don't understand why we're here," my mother repeated every five minutes, "we're not crazy."

"That's not what this is about," the therapist earnestly tried to assure her, growing increasingly uneasy and alarmed as my mother angrily accused her of accusing us all of being mentally ill, thus ensuring that the therapist believed we were.

My father did not say a word, refusing to answer any of the therapist's questions, refusing even to look her in the eye. He sat silently in the chair, staring at the floor the entire time.

"Are you satisfied?" my mother screamed in the car all the way home. "Are you? Are you happy now?"

"Never do that to us again," my father joined in. "It was horrible."

The letter I got from the therapist a few weeks later was the final blow: she had failed to convince her supervisor that my parents should not be part of my therapy. And since my parents had refused to participate, she couldn't treat me anymore.

It was just another rejection, just another loss, just another brick wall. I hadn't really expected it to work. I was a million years older than she would ever be.

It was during this period that I got the last beating I would ever get from my mother. She was a serious face-slapper when I was small but by my teen years had switched to full frontal assaults, flying at me with arms flailing. She was a tiny woman, chubby and non-athletic, and had the upper body strength of a ten-year-old so I found the flailing much easier to take than the face-slapping, which used to leave me in a tearful rage.

But one night in late winter, I quietly let myself into the house and came face to face with her, hovering like an angry wraith in a pink frilly nightgown. I was often late for the general curfew they set, but this time, it was nearly 4 a.m., a good three hours late, which was unusual even for me. Things had run overtime at Mona's that night, owing mainly to a giant bird that took forever to cook, and the wine we consumed to ease our hungry impatience, which then required a nap and then a lot of coffee before it was safe for her to drive me home. I assumed they'd never know, since they were usually sound asleep when I came in.

"Whore!" she flailed. "Tramp! Where were you all night? Who were you with?"

I kept walking. She followed me, punching my back, but I kept going until I got into my room, where I climbed into bed with all my clothes still on and pulled the blanket up over my head. Now she beat me on top of the blanket, wildly striking all over my torso and head. I didn't move. I let her flail. I opened my eyes under the blanket and tried to feel something. I couldn't. There was nothing to feel. Nothing hurt. Even if it hurt it didn't hurt. I wasn't really there. I was watching a girl under a blanket be beaten by a deranged woman. I had no opinion about it. I probably deserved it. But not for the reasons she thought. I deserved it because I hated her. I hated everything about her. I was a horrible, horrible child. Though I wasn't, because the real me was a million miles away, glumly waiting for the beating to stop so I could go to sleep.

It didn't matter, did it? It couldn't matter. If I allowed it to matter then the center fell out of my life and I couldn't go on. Nothing mattered. Only Mona mattered.

I was now spending every weekend with her, and saw her as many times during the week as her work schedule allowed. We couldn't get enough of each other's company, though clouds seemed to overhang us at times. Neither of us was truly happy. We only made up a form of happiness when we were together. It wasn't always enough.

One weekend, on one of those nights when we were both so overwrought we carried our endless dialogue into the bedroom, we hopped into the bed together to continue chattering until we passed out. Or so I thought. Long before we ran out of conversation, Mona kissed me full on the lips. I immediately kissed her back with a smile. It was so nice finally to kiss her deeply on her lips. We started making out and I crushed her full, round body in my arms. Within seconds, she had slid herself under me so I was lying on top of her. I pulled her t-shirt up to see her plump breasts, softly cupping them to raise them to my mouth.

She slid a finger into my cunt. I was so surprised, I gasped and recoiled, but then I relaxed again. A woman's finger in my pussy felt different from a man's – smaller, with a much lighter touch. She played with my pussy as I sucked her nipples, and began humping her while she moaned beneath me.

"I'm making love to Mona!" the words kept replaying in my head. I didn't know how I felt. Did this mean we would be lesbians now, and would have sex for the rest of our lives? I could do that for Mona, for the sake of Mona, for the sake of love. I could. I loved her. Even if it didn't feel the way it felt with men, even if it didn't make me hungry for an orgasm, it felt like pure love seeping into me. I could live for that pure love. I could.

I kissed her a thousand times, her face, her neck, her breasts and belly, too shy to go any further, and then rubbing against her, burying my nose in her thick dark hair. She smelled so familiar, so sweet, and her flesh was like being wrapped in heaven.

In the morning, I kissed her passionately.

She said, "We can never do that again."

"What? Why?"

"We're not lesbians," she said, "I'm not a lesbian." She laughed uneasily. "I don't want to open that can of worms."

"I just thought..." I was so confused, I faltered. "I just thought it was a natural extension of our love. I mean..."

She cut me off. "It was! That's what it was. But if we do it again, we'll be lesbians."

I knew she was wrong but I wasn't going to argue. I felt an incredible sense of disappointment – her body was so beautiful to me, the feeling of being all wrapped up with her had been so comforting. It wasn't fair to give me that and then snatch it away, or to act as if our beautiful moment was, in fact, a shameful one. But it didn't matter. It didn't change the feelings that drove us to express our love. It wasn't about sex for us anyway. It was about a truer kind of love.

What did matter was that Mona called me a few days later in tears, telling me that Chloe had done something so awful that Mona had kicked her out and demanded she get all her stuff gone by the end of the week.

Chloe had slipped so far into the background for me that when I thought about her now, it was only to secretly hope she would move out so that I could move in. A turning point in my relationship with her came when she told me of an affair she was having at work with a married man. They were having their liaisons at the office. One day, a co-worker on her way to the Xerox machine found them fucking doggie-style in a stairwell. Both of them lost their jobs. That Chloe had, first, knowingly carried on with a married guy, and second, didn't even know how to do it discreetly, made me lose respect for her. Plus, the escapade put her back on the dole with Mona and that much further from moving out.

What tipped Mona over the edge was Chloe's current flame. He was a biker who came by in full leathers. Mona thought he was scary trash and did not want him in her house. She asked Chloe not to bring him around too much, but when he got kicked out of his place, Chloe begged Mona to let him stay for a week or two and moved him into her bed before Mona had a chance to turn her down.

Mona called me late at night to whisper about how uncomfortable the situation made her. He was arrogant and rude, and Chloe acted crazy when she was with him. I didn't understand what she meant until she called me late one night in a panic.

"I can't take anymore," Mona said. "I'm kicking them out. Chloe was screaming and screaming like he was killing her."

I started giggling. "Yeah, well, I guess they're hot for each other."

"No, you don't understand. I heard the sounds of him hitting her. Slaps! I heard slaps."

"Oh no, what?"

"So I went into the living room and he was beating her."

"Holy shit, he abuses her?" I was horrified.

"Well, yes. But," Mona hesitated for a long moment, then whispered, "she wanted it. He was smacking her ass and she liked it." Mona paused in stunned silence. "She told me to go back to my room, she was into it!"

OH!!!!!! OH! They were doing sadomasochistic things in bed!! OH! They were kinky! I was speechless.

"They have to go," she said with finality. "I'm not putting up with that! No way!"

"Really? I mean, if they both like it..."

"It's sick!" she said. "The whole thing is sick. I don't want that in my home."

I didn't know what to say. If Mona knew what I jerked off about every night, she would feel the same contempt for me. Combined with her requirement that we never get sexual again, I was starting to wonder if she loved the real me at all.

"I gave her until Friday to get out," Mona said. "They said they'd leave tomorrow, and go stay with his sister."

This was my opportunity. With Chloe gone, there was room for me now. I knew Mona didn't want a permanent roommate but there was ROOM FOR ME. I couldn't restrain myself, I had to ask.

"So... what will you do with the spare bed in the living room?" I asked coyly. "Think you want another roommate?"

"Fuck no," Mona said. "I'm never having another roommate. I cannot wait to have my place back to myself! I'm done with roommates. What a disaster, right?"

"Right," I said. "Yeah, what a disaster."

She'd never promised me I could move in. I never directly asked about it. It didn't even occur to her as she said those words that her best friend would feel utterly rejected. Or did she? She knew what I was going through at home. She knew how desperately I needed to leave. She had promised to marry me!

I didn't know where I stood with her anymore. She didn't seem to know where she stood with me either because once Chloe moved out, Mona got inexplicably busy and the weekend invitations grew fewer. When I asked for specifics, she was vague. When I got frustrated, she told me to come over. Once I was there, she acted as though nothing had changed. Except everything had.

I was brooding over Mona on a bench in the little park across from school one cold January day when Dane sauntered past, his book bag slung over his shoulder.

"You look like you just lost your best friend." He peered down at me. "I'd take you for a drink, but I have another class to teach."

A shock went down my spine. "I'd go with you for a drink," I said.

"Yeah? I have this class. Would you wait for me? In the library?"

"Yes," I said, "yes, I will wait."

I couldn't believe what was happening. It was the chance I'd been living for.

Dane drove me to the library across from his class building, parked, and then walked me to the library's poetry reading room.

"Do you have something to read?" he asked.

I pulled *Paradise Lost* out of my book bag. "I'm behind on Milton. I'll be fine."

The minute he left, I ran to the phone bank and called Mona.

"Mona, Mona, I'm still at school. Dane asked me out for a drink!"

Mona did not seem as excited as I thought she'd be. We hung up quickly and I went back to Milton. The lines had a strange effect on me. It was impossible to focus on them but when I managed to read a line, its impact was dramatic. The more I read, the more emotional I became. I raced back to the phones.

"Mona, I'm reading Milton, and it's making me feel so much!"

This time Mona ended the call abruptly, saying she had something on the stove.

I sat down with Milton once more in wonder. Again, the text lit up. He was so true. He saw so much with blind eyes. Every word was like a beacon, and every one led me closer to my destiny with Dane. OMG, Dane was finally taking me out. My new life with him was about to begin! OMG. Dane! Dane was my salvation!!! My knight in shining armor! I always knew HE, HIM, THAT MAN would come to me!

I called Mona again. "I can't believe Dane wants to have a drink with me."

"Listen, I'm cooking. Could you call me back tomorrow? After something actually happens? This is too much stress."

She hung up on me and I returned to my books, having epiphanies over every line I read.

My real life is about to begin, I kept thinking, *my real life has arrived! We'll travel to Mallorca and Istanbul and Rome, and not in that order, and we'll live in a sunny apartment on the Upper West Side where I'll write poetry and he'll hold me in his arms every night.*

I was cosmically vibrating by the time Dane returned.

"I need a drink," he said. He gave me a closer look. "You look like you really need one."

He packed me back in his car, and drove to a better neighborhood, where he spotted a bar. We sat down and he ordered for us both, scotch for him and a martini for me. I sipped it obediently though it tasted like gasoline. I twitched and wiggled across from him while he savored his scotch. I wished I'd taken a longer shower that morning. I wished I'd put on make-up that day. I wished I didn't have so many pimples. I wished I'd spent more time on my hair. I wished I'd worn a better outfit and shoes with a bigger heel so I didn't look like such a pipsqueak when I walked next to him.

"Gloria," he leaned in, gazing at me with an intimidatingly meaningful look.

My heart dropped to my shoes. He saw through me. I knew it. Next would come a long speech about how I had to quit pestering him, and how disappointed he was that my work wasn't as good as it could be, and how I never lived up to my potential, and how my grade would be lower than expected. That's why he brought me here: to get me drunk and let me down easy.

"Gloria, you're the most attractive woman I've ever met," he blurted. "There," he said as he took another gulp, "I finally said it."

I gaped at him and he looked equally surprised: I don't know which one of us was more taken aback by his confession.

He said he found me attractive. How was that possible? For almost two years now I'd been relentlessly stalking him and suddenly he found me attractive? When and how did it happen? Was our life together really beginning now? Maybe I wouldn't even have to go home, maybe I could just run away with him tonight. Oh my fucking God. YES!!!

Two hours later, we were driving up to a motel out by the JFK International Airport called Jade East. I hadn't told him how I felt about him. I didn't know how to. Going to a motel seemed like the next logical step after we both had a couple of drinks but as soon as we arrived, I didn't want to be there. This wasn't what I'd wanted, this cliché encounter in a squalid short-stay motel off the highway. That's not what I wanted with the man I worshiped. But there I was, in a skanky dive with other cheaters, liars, and whores, while the love of my life paid cash to the clerk and tried to pretend we weren't really there together.

He removed his clothes without discussion and hopped under the blankets. I removed mine and joined him. It felt so wrong, so brutal, so inhibited. At first touch, his body felt strange to me, not comforting, not what I liked. I could not adjust my motor to his speed. When he got on top of me to fuck me missionary style, without foreplay or seductions, I became every woman I'd seen in porn movies. The less excited I was, the louder I seemed to groan. I couldn't stop myself. I needed to prove to him, to myself, that this was the best, most wonderful fucking of my life.

He barely made a sound when he came and though I'd pretended to cum several times, I hadn't cum at all and felt relieved when he rolled off of me. He got up from the bed and sank into the chair beside it. He looked depressed.

"Did I make too much noise?" I said, "I'm sorry, I... I guess I really got carried away by how good you were," I lied, unwilling to admit to myself that we had no chemistry.

He shook his head ruefully. "I wasn't that good." He dressed quickly, then sat on the edge of the bed.

"I feel like everything is falling apart," he said. He dropped his face into his hands and sat there, bent over. "It's all falling apart. My life. Everything. It's like a wall crashed in on me tonight, and it's still crashing on the inside."

I wanted to help him, but this was the first time a grown man had fallen apart on me. I didn't know how to put him back together. In fact, I was a little angry about it. He was thirty-nine. He was supposed to know shit. He was supposed to know shit better than I knew shit, and he was supposed to be able to handle shit, because he was an adult. It wasn't fair that he was dumping his shit on me. In all my fantasies, he was the one who had all the answers.

"I can't deal with this," I whispered.

He stiffened and stood up. "Yeah. I know," he said. "Let's get the fuck out of here."

He drove me home to Sheepshead Bay in silence. Just blocks before my parents' house, he delivered a death blow. "We can't do this again."

"What do you mean?" Despite the disappointment of it all, I thought it was a stupid fumble, not a fiasco. I clung to the hope that it was only the awkward beginning to our epic romance, something we'd laugh about in years to come.

"It's just not right for a man of my age to sleep with someone your age. We can't sleep together."

"But we just did," I said.

"We shouldn't have done what we did."

"You can't change what happened." I refused to believe what I was hearing. I could not accept that my night of love had turned into a tawdry nightmare. I loved him. I loved him more than I'd ever loved any man, and I loved him for all the right reasons, didn't I? I certainly didn't love him for his cock.

"I don't want to start something I can't finish," he said.

"But we already started."

"That's why it has to stop," he said. "What are you, seventeen?"

"I'm almost nineteen."

"Right. I'm old enough to be your father."

We pulled up to the house and he leaned in to kiss my forehead goodbye.

"No," I said as I pushed him away. I ran from the car, not looking over my shoulder, afraid that right then and there, I would literally die.

But I did not die as I climbed the stairs, nor did my heart burst when I got into bed. I cried. I cried a lot. I was not angry at him. I was angry at life. I was angry at myself, for how I lied to him, pretending to have orgasms when I was barely wet. And now – now there was nothing to live for. I'd lost my chance with him. I probably scared him with my screams. I closed my eyes, and prepared to die of a broken heart during the night, tears still running down my cheeks.

When I woke up the next day, and saw that I was alive, I knew what I had to do. I had to move the fuck out. I had to get my shit together. I was on my own. It was like my parents always warned me, you can never rely on anyone.

I had to forget about everyone who was slowing me down and focus on finding a place to live so I could move out when classes were done. My real life, the life that mattered, couldn't begin until then. As long as I lived in my parents' home, my life would be poisoned.

Although the temperature had changed between us, when the spring of 1974 came, I settled into a regular pattern of spending weekends at Mona's. She never invited me to chat in her bed again, so the question of our latent lesbianism was put away, but the love was still strong.

I was spending a quiet afternoon at her place one Sunday when the phone rang. My mother, who rarely called, was on the other end. She wanted me to come home immediately. By the tone of her voice, I knew another vicious drama would explode if I didn't immediately cede. When I showed up, she was waiting for me on the porch.

"What's the matter?"

"You're killing us!" She pushed me into the house. "You're killing your father!"

"What are you talking about?"

"Daddy had to go to emergency. It's all your fault."

"What do you mean?"

"He almost had a heart attack."

"What do you mean?" I kept repeating, not understanding how I had caused it. "What did I do?"

I ran to their bedroom to see him for myself. He was sitting on the bed, staring into space.

"Dad? Are you okay?"

His eyes were vague. His legs dangled over the edge of the bed, like a child.

"Dad?"

"Don't talk to him!" My mother charged in and forced me out of the room.

"What's wrong with him?"

"You have to ask why you're breaking your father's heart?" my mother snapped. As she saw it, if I was a good Jewish daughter, I'd already know what a bad Jewish daughter I really was.

By dinner time, everything was back to normal, and neither of my parents wanted to talk to me about what had transpired while I was away.

Two weeks later, I was at a new part-time job, typing invoices in a shirt factory in the garment district, when my mother called. Since I was a part-time, temporary worker, the boss gave me the stink eye and a brief lecture on company policy before he handed me the receiver.

"What's the matter, Mom." I was really scared. She had never, ever, called me at a job before.

"I want you should come home now," she said.

I dragged the cord as far away from my frowning boss as possible. "Mom, I told you I was working today. What happened? Is Daddy ok?"

"You'll come straight home after work?"

"Yes, I'll be there at six. What happened?"

She was mollified. "OK, I'll tell you when you get here. Six o'clock. Remember you promised."

I raced home from work to find her padding around the kitchen in her pink apron and matching slippers. She looked at the clock. "It's just six. You made good time."

"Well??"

"Well, what?"

"You called me at work. I thought something happened!"

"Since when can't a mother call her daughter at work?" She looked at me reproachfully. "Go wash up, and set the table before your father gets home."

The more irrational my parents got, the blurrier life seemed. I stayed in my bedroom, watching television, sometimes sitting up all night until it was time to leave for school in the morning. There was no point seeing Mona. I was afraid to stay out for overnights, lest my father fall ill with his mystery illness. I was afraid to be home, because peace of mind was impossible with my mother around. When I told my mother I wanted to install a latch on my bedroom door, the battle which ensued escalated until my father came racing in, red in the face.

"You're killing your mother," he said. "Don't you see what you're doing? You're killing her!"

"She says I'm killing you, you say I'm killing her," I said. "What the hell is going on, what are you even talking about?"

It hurt me that they thought I was trying to hurt them. As much as I disliked my mother's behavior, I didn't want to hurt either of my parents. But I didn't want them to hurt me either and it seemed like they could not help themselves.

Sometime in April, my mother cleared the dinner table and said we needed to talk.

"You know," she said, "your parents are your best friends. We're the ones who love you. The only ones who really love you."

I'd heard this before. They hammered the theme home to me as a child, that when push came to shove, the only ones I could ever trust was them. I'd grown up since then. I'd learned that people did care for me. Or at least they didn't treat me as bad as my mother did. But I bowed my head and listened, wondering where this was going.

"There's nothing you can't tell us," my mother said. "Nothing. We are the only ones you can trust. You should tell us everything."

"Everything," my father echoed. "There should be no secrets."

This statement floored me. This was the house of secrets. Our family dynamics were built on secrets and things you couldn't tell someone and things you'd twist to cover your own ass and things you would never say with others around and things you'd deny in public.

"What do you mean, no secrets?"

"Are you a virgin?" my mother asked.

"What?" A sharp stab of guilt seared my gut. They didn't want to know. I knew they didn't want to know. But I was sick of lying. "No. Not since last year," I lied anyway, quickly deciding to count from Raph and to use the traditional definition of virginity as someone sticking their dick inside me, and not all the handjobs and blowjobs, which were, by then, literally uncountable anyway. If I told them I actually fucked at age fourteen, the whole world would explode.

"Was it Mona?" she screamed. "At her apartment?"

"Mona?" I almost laughed out loud. "How? No, no, it was last year with a college professor. That college professor I was so close to, you know, Raph."

Facts were that I was a pretty good student and a mostly obedient daughter, who had part-time jobs and did lots of chores at home. Was I killing them because I was sexually active? Was that what they were trying to say?

"I heard something!" my father bellowed. He jumped up from the table and ran to the back of the house, where we heard him go out to the back patio.

"I have to go see!" my mother cried, and ran after him.

I sat alone at the table, waiting for them to return. They didn't. After ten minutes, I went out to the back patio, anxious they'd both be dead on the floor, a suicide note beside them, scribbled in my mother's hand, saying, *"It's Gloria's fault."* But no, they were just sitting in folding chairs.

"Well?" I asked. "What the hell?"

Their entire emotional temperature had changed again.

"Well, what?" my mother said.

"We were having a conversation..."

"Daddy thought he heard a lightbulb break," she said. "But it didn't."

"A lightbulb?"

She walked back into the house. "Who wants fruit?"

I looked at my father. He wouldn't meet my eyes. "Dad? What the hell was that?"

He went back inside without a word.

I sat on the back patio alone for a few hours, staring down at the postage-stamp backyard and rows of houses where happier families lived. What more proof did I need that this was a madhouse? Once upon a time, I thought my dad was an ally. He was always kinder and more loving than my mother. Now she had completely poisoned him, cut off his balls, turned him into someone he never was: frightened. He was too frightened of his wife even to love his daughter the way a father should.

The subject of my virginity was never mentioned again. My mother seemed content that I was now staying home most of the time, and acted friendlier than before, gloating over my seeming defeat. One night, I heard my mother excitedly talking in Polish to someone overseas. I knew they were far away because my mother always raised her voice when she talked to foreign countries, as if screaming into the phone would make it easier for people on the other side to hear her.

"That was Lena!" she said as she burst into my room.

Lena was one of her childhood friends, someone she'd gone to school with as a girl and survived the war with as a teenager. She visited us once when I was a child. Lena had dyed blond hair and exaggerated mannerisms. Every morning, she ran in place in the living room, wearing a thin nightie and holding her breasts in her hands like cannons, the nipples pointed at me. When I asked her why she did that, she told me, in broken English, that they would hit her in the head otherwise. It was logical but it sounded very unpleasant. That was all I remembered about Lena.

"You said you wanted to go to Paris," my mother said. "I talked to Lena and you can stay with her in Paris."

This was news to me. Of course I wanted to go to Paris. Doesn't everyone? I vaguely remembered once screaming that "If I had the money, I'd get out of this asylum and go to Europe tomorrow!" It didn't mean I was ready to go this summer or that Paris was my first choice. I didn't even have a passport. Besides, I couldn't afford to go. I was just weeks away from my financial goal of two months' rent, plus a cushion for other bills and emergencies.

"When?" I asked.

"July," she said, "go for four weeks. Think of it as a gift from us." She beamed. "Lena has a big apartment, you can have your own bedroom."

"I have to think about it."

"What's to think about? It's a present!"

I was thinking about the cost of travel. Even with my parents footing the fare, and their friend providing housing and food, I'd still end up spending if I wanted to see anything or eat out, and I wouldn't be able to earn any money during those weeks.

On the other hand, if I didn't take my parents' offer, it might never come around again, especially after I moved out. Besides, what did I have to stay for? My life was falling apart around me. My beautiful dream about Dane was annihilated. He didn't want me. Mona didn't want me either, not the real me. No one did. But I was stuck with me so I had to think about what I needed, which was to get the fuck away from my parents, so they couldn't keeping blaming me for their own unhappiness.

I phoned Mona for her advice. "Out of the blue, my parents offered me a trip to Europe this summer, do you think I should go?"

"Summer's just a few weeks away. You can't get ready in time," she said.

"I can do it," I said. "I'll find a way. The question is whether I should." I hesitated. "Should I go, Mona? Should I leave for a month?"

She answered slowly. "I'll miss you. But it's Europe. I guess you have to go." She paused. "I'd go if someone else was paying."

I called for advice but what I really wanted was her to beg me to stay, to tell me she couldn't stand being without me for a month, to make leaving her so painful that I'd stand strong against my mother's emotional blackmail. Instead, she seemed a little sad, but nothing that a bottle of wine with a new man couldn't fix.

"I love you, Mona," I said.

"I love you too," she said. "Don't sound so bummed. I'll be here when you get back."

Her words made the decision for me. I was going. I was getting the fuck out of hell.

I paid a fee to accelerate the passport process and got it in no time. Through a student travel organization, I found an insanely cheap deal to sail on the Queen Elizabeth II to Europe, then return by plane. In a week's time, I had everything lined up neatly. The day I had to pay for my tickets, I asked my mother for the promised money. She went to the cigar box she kept in her dresser and removed a handful of bills.

"We're only paying for half," she said. I stared at her uncomprehendingly. How could half of what I needed be enough to get what I needed. "You have money in savings, you can use that for the rest."

And then I understood. I understood everything, even how I was killing them. All of it had been leading up to this moment. All the drama and illnesses, all the times she stirred up trouble, it had all led up to this moment. She'd been gas-lighting me and my father while counting up my earnings in her head all along, calculating what I had, even asking to look at my bankbook, which I naïvely showed her, thinking she was proud that I was saving for the future. Instead, she'd been plotting all along how to thwart my plans to move out. God knows what lies she told my father about me, what lies she'd told me about him. She was ruthless and crude and mean.

Fuck her. I was going. This ship was departing in ten days. I was going to be on it. I couldn't stay in her home another minute. I couldn't stand the sight of my mother now.

"Will you throw in a little extra for expenses, like food?" I asked.

"OK," she said. "I can do that. I'll give it to you the day you leave."

"Fine," I said.

I got the money out of my bank and bought my tickets and got a haircut and packed my bags and said my goodbyes to my friends and made it to my departure date feeling cold inside, ice cold. Whatever happened next, I'd figure it out. I would go to France and I would fuck a maximum of men and see a maximum of sights and drink a maximum of wine, and when I came back, I would move out anyway, money or no, because I would do anything, literally anything, to get away from her now.

I was going to Paris to drink up the world. My real life, my beautiful life, was out there and I was going to find it. I was on my own journey now. I'd survive. I was the most surviving bitch the world had ever seen.

Dr. Gloria Brame is best known for her books *Different Loving* and *The Truth About Sex* (trilogy), which promote evidence-based, pro-diversity perspectives on human sexuality. A clinical sex therapist and much sought-after expert on the biopsychology of sex, Gloria has been a  leader in radical sex theory and education since 1987, when she founded the world's first online BDSM support group. Gloria's previous memoir was *Naked Memory: Confessions of a Sexual Revolutionary*. The long-awaited follow-up to *Different Loving* will be available before the end of 2015.

CPSIA information can be obtained
at www.ICGtesting.com
Printed in the USA
LVOW03s0540120917
548367LV00022B/1185/P